Missio Politica

This book is written with passion and authenticity. *Missio Politica* combines deep theological scholarship and thinking from a variety of disciplines ranging from political thought to social anthropology. It is packed with practical wisdom gained from the author's in-depth experience of social and political engagement from the grassroots level upwards. The result is a challenging and inspiring call to radical discipleship that is as academically rigorous as it is practical. It is a must-read for anyone wanting to grow in their understanding of what it means to be a faithful disciple of Jesus and servant of the King of Kings.

Mark Galpin, PhD
Tutor and Lecturer, All Nations Christian College, Ware, UK

This book by Johannes Reimer provides in-depth theological reflection as well as practical guidelines for Christian mission that understands the transformation of communities to be the comprehensive reversal of the effects of sin over all of life and all the earth that alienated men and women from God, from self, from others and from the environment. The author makes it clear that God's intention for his church is to be his instrument in restoring human beings to be full bearers of his image and bring back his order to creation. The task of God's people begins in this life but will only be completed when Christ returns in glory at the end of time.

Professor P. J. (Flip) Buys, ThD
International Director, World Reformed Fellowship

The great value of this book is its wide-ranging practicality. Johannes Reimer draws on his experience of mission in communist Eastern and capitalist Western Europe, as well as his studies in South Africa during that country's apartheid era, to challenge Christians everywhere to an authentic, contextual and biblically-shaped engagement with the powers of this age.

Vinoth Ramachandra, PhD
International Secretary for Dialogue & Social Engagement, IFES, Sri Lanka

Has there ever been a time in church history when our understanding of the links between mission and political engagement has been more essential? Through this excellent book, Johannes helps unpack the clear biblical mandate that followers of Jesus can never be apolitical. Using examples from across the globe, this book moves beyond theory and gives practical examples of what it means for the church to be truly transformative in its communities. A must-read for church leaders, community development practitioners, and all Christians who are serious about mission.

Matthew Maury
CEO, TEAR Australia

Missio Politica: The Mission of the Church and Politics meets a crying need in the Christian church today on knowing why and how followers of Christ should be meaningfully involved in politics as mission. It is essential reading for missional congregations – thorough, comprehensive, and Word-centered. The book is a fine blend between academic and practical helps. There is a refreshing honesty in dealing with an issue that unfortunately divides twenty-first century believers – politics and the church's mission.

Rev CB Samuel
Advisor for Micah Global
Former CEO of the Evangelical Fellowship of India Commission on Relief
Itinerant Theologian and Bible Teacher

"Jesus is Lord." This highly charged political statement is at the heart of Johannes Reimer's book on the church and politics. Drawing us into the biblical narratives, from God's calling of a people Israel to the scattering after Pentecost, Reimer carefully examines the ways in which God's people engage in the political world and how our participation in the Triune God's mission entails being part of the struggles for justice, peace and reconciliation. In a world that longs to hear and see the good news of the gospel, this book reminds all Christians of our call to be and to share that good news in the world today.

C. Rosalee Velloso Ewell, PhD
Principal, Redcliffe College, Gloucester, UK
Executive Director, Theological Commission of the World Evangelical Alliance

This is the sort of book on politics written by an evangelical Christian that I am very glad to recommend for two reasons. One reason is that it is written by a person who has been able to pay the price for living according to his biblically based Christian convictions in a situation in which he had no other choice if he wanted to be faithful to the Lord Jesus Christ. In the second place, I wholeheartedly recommend this book because the challenge that Johannes Reimer met in his own situation is a very common challenge in most countries in today´s world. I hope and pray that *Missio Politica* will encourage many readers to make a whole-hearted commitment to the politics of the kingdom of God and his justice.

C. René Padilla, PhD
Ecuadorian Evangelical Theologian and Missiologist
Founder of Kairos
President Emeritus, Micah Global

Missio Politica

The Mission of Church and Politics

Johannes Reimer

micah
global

Langham
GLOBAL LIBRARY

© 2017 by Johannes Reimer

Published 2017 by Langham Global Library
An imprint of Langham Creative Projects

Langham Partnership
PO Box 296, Carlisle, Cumbria CA3 9WZ, UK
www.langham.org

Published in partnership with Micah Global

Micah Global
PO Box 381, Carlisle, CA1 9FE, United Kingdom
www.micahglobal.org

ISBNs:
978-1-78368-351-2 Print
978-1-78368-352-9 ePub
978-1-78368-353-6 Mobi
978-1-78368-354-3 PDF

British Library Cataloguing in Publication Data
A catalogue record for this book is available from the British Library

ISBN: 978-1-78368-351-2

Cover & Book Design: projectluz.com

Dedicated to the late Professor Dr Willem A. Saayman

CONTENTS

Foreword

I first met Johannes Reimer back in 2010 at the Christian Community Development Conference held every two years in Germany. We were jointly responsible for facilitating a workshop on integral mission and holistic ministry. It was here I first heard Johannes speak on the missional cycle and recognized in this approach a similarity with Micah's[1] application teachings. Johannes has written extensively on this subject, and his books are available for all those who speak German. We hope they will all be available in English soon, as what he discusses in these books is critical for all of us to wrestle with. I am thrilled to see *Missio Politica* completed: Johannes touches on a number of these approaches in this book as he explores mission and politics. As with all Johannes says and does, *Missio Politica* inspires God's church to re-read Scripture with a missional lens and gives us practical examples of how to respond within our own communities and contexts.

A well-meaning pastor in Haiti confronted me in a Micah National Integral Mission Conversation after I had presented a reflection on what the term *ecclesia* meant – *a people called out to take responsibility for their community*. I had unpacked this through God's missional agenda, sharing the Micah Integral Mission definition to help explore what this looks like in practice:

> Integral mission or holistic transformation is the proclamation and demonstration of the gospel.
>
> It is not simply that evangelism and social involvement are to be done alongside each other. Rather, in integral mission, our proclamation has social consequences as we call people to love and repentance in all areas of life, and our social involvement has evangelistic consequences as we bear witness to the transforming grace of Jesus Christ. (Micah Declaration on Integral Mission, September 2001)

This pastor was adamant that the church had been called to seek God's kingdom first (Matt 6:33) – that this alone was our responsibility. His argument was that our main aim in life was to get to heaven – so spiritual salvation was

---

1. Micah Global is an international network for integral mission. See: http://www.micahnetwork.org (Last access: 23 August 2017).

the priority and heaven the destination (a place not in any way associated with the world).

This led me to unpack what God meant by seeking the kingdom of God and seeking his righteousness.

Seeking the Kingdom of God

It is clear from our study of the Bible and especially the way Jesus spoke of the kingdom of God that he is not referring to a specific geographical location. Rather he is referring to the reign of God. You can't have a kingdom without a king, and we all acknowledge that the King of kings is Jesus Christ.

The kingdom of God is not referring to a future destination only – Jesus clearly stated that the kingdom of God was here now, among us. The kingdom of God is a present reality now.

Speaking of a king and a kingdom is political language. It implies a number of important points:

1. **Authority**: Jesus is king over all the earth – all nations, all of creation. His reign is everlasting and his dominion is over everyone and everything.

2. **Covenantal**: God is king over his people. In the Old Testament God calls out a people to demonstrate his character and purpose to all nations. In the New Testament Jesus calls out a people (*ecclesia* – his church) to demonstrate a new humanity, his kingdom. God promises to walk with his *ecclesia* and sends them to fulfil his purpose, his mission. As their King and Lord he provides for them and requires obedience from them, so that all may see and know his name and his love. The church is God's ambassador representing his kingdom as well as his servants, serving all in his name. An ambassador is a political calling, and a priestly role is a serving and discipling role.

3. **Messianic**: the future anticipation of when God would become king. The expectation of change when Jesus comes is: the end of war, the presence of peace and justice, and of life in all its fullness. The kingdom coming would reverse all the injustices in the world. We know that Jesus is the expected Messiah and had inaugurated the new kingdom already when he came. We know that all the injustices, pain, and suffering were not removed when Jesus walked on earth,

though we saw evidence of this in and through all he did and taught. Jesus explained that the kingdom of God was:

a. Like a seed: growing up among us and in us
b. Like yeast: rising up through the bread
c. Like a net: reaching into the water to collect the fish

There is already evidence of the kingdom of God as we his people live out his mission, demonstrate his kingdom in all its aspects. There is also the tension of the not yet – the reality that the full aspect of the kingdom will also be revealed when Christ returns.

Seeking His Righteousness

This means being in a right relationship with God, accepting him as Lord and Saviour. Recognizing and then living out a right relationship with God in obedience to his call – his mission. Being in Christ and living a right relationship with him compels us to seek right relationships among people through justice.

So, seeking the kingdom of God and his righteousness does not take us out of the world, but quite the opposite: it puts us into the world to tangibly live out the kingdom of God. We do this through walking in a right relationship with God, becoming more and more like Jesus, so that we can obediently follow all that God commands and demonstrate the love of God to all nations.

Seeking his righteousness is also about seeking justice for all people, for his creation.

Missio Politica helps us to understand what seeking justice looks like through the Old Testament and the New Testament, and unpacks both theologically and practically how we can live this out in our community.

We recognize that we can never separate our faith from our politics. Seeking first the kingdom of God and his righteousness and justice means we make this a fundamental priority in all of our life. We live by the truth that God reigns. It requires a radical discipleship, seeking to model his justice in all aspects of life and earnestly working toward seeking his justice for all.

Missio Politica inspires us to do just that.

Sheryl Haw
International Director, Micah Global

Abbreviations

BoL	Beginning of Life
CCD	Christian Community Development
CD	Community Development
CACD	Catalytic-Activating Community Development
CCIA	Church's Commission on Internal Affairs
CCM	Christian Community Mediation
CPM	Church-Planting Movement
ESJ	Evangelicals for Social Justice
IMC	International Missionary Council
LCC	Lithuania Christian College
LCWE	Lausanne Committee for World Evangelization
LttW	Light to the World
NSCC	New Song Community Church
USSR	Union of the Soviet Socialist Republics
WCC	World Council of Churches
WEA	World Evangelical Alliance
WWII	World War II

1

Introduction

1.1. A Personal Search

I grew up in a communist country, and I am from a nonconformist church tradition. Politically active before coming to Christ, I was carefully discipled to withdraw from all political activity once I became a Christian. "The church of Christ is by her nature apolitical," my pastor taught me. "Politically active Christians will soon compromise their faith," he added, "because politics is all about compromise. Politics is a dirty business. Our words shall be yes yes and no no, as Jesus advised us. Compromise is in principle evil." So I followed my pastor's advice on this matter.

Soon all my non-Christian friends distanced themselves from me, and I left the public arena, except for some provocative evangelistic actions. When the time came to do military service, I refused to do so because of my nonconformist theological convictions.[1] Persecution, imprisonment, and labour camp followed. My persecutors argued I was badly treated because of my political actions in refusing to do military service.

It was during this time of imprisonment that I consciously started to rethink my convictions regarding political involvement. I had withdrawn from politically motivated behaviour and in the process had automatically become a political activist. At least in the eyes of the government. It was easy for me to recollect many other stories in which our church was blamed for undermining the political *status quo* in our country. In fact, none of my fellow brothers and sisters were imprisoned because of their faith in Christ. The official reading was always politically subversive behaviour. Our faith seemed to create trouble. No,

---

1. See the story in Johannes Reimer, *Liberty in Confinement: Faith Story in the Red Army* (Winnipeg: Kindred Press, 2000).

1

we did not join political parties. We withdrew from any political responsibility. And yet, wherever our lives where involved in the public sphere, the public reacted. We did not join in with corrupt behaviour, and we did not cheat others to gain more for ourselves. When asked to witness wrongdoing, we spoke the truth. In a culture of lies this was highly, politically incorrect.

Are the "politically incorrect" politically involved? Is presenting an alternative lifestyle to society a political statement? Questions like this came to mind and forced me to think through the issues. During this process of thinking about political activity as a Christian, the political powers in the USSR made life for me and my family miserable and unbearable, so we fled the country.

Once in the West I was free to ask my questions. And I was rather surprised as I observed my Western Christian brothers and sisters. Many of them acted in full disagreement with my pastor at home. They consciously joined political parties. Prominent politicians confessed their faith in Jesus Christ, and I found books on the social and political involvement of the church. There seemed to be an amazing freedom to accept political activity. Sure, some Christians in the West seemed as critical as my own home church, and it became obvious that there was vast disagreement on the issue. On the other hand, it did not take very long to discover how little effect the "Christian element" had on our political life. Christians involved in politics, when asked why they did what they did, would seldom argue theologically. It seemed that such arguments rarely existed. In some instances, Christians in politics behaved even worse than non-Christians.

I was left with more questions than ever before. Does the church of Christ have a political mandate? And if so, how is such a mandate biblically justified? It took me years to answer this question. This essay is a short summary of my findings.

1.2. You Can't Sit at Home and Wait

My personal search for answers was intensified in 1991. Lithuania, a Soviet Republic, declared independence from the USSR and was severely under threat from the Moscow-ruled Soviet-regime. A friend of mine called me one day and said: "You can't sit home, Johannes, and do nothing. Our people are fighting for freedom. They need our support."

His telephone call woke me up. I would not go to Lithuania, pick up arms and fight for freedom, but I could go and pray for the people. My presence in the country would not make any crucial difference in how the Soviets related to the small Baltic country, but I could preach to the Lithuanians and lead them to Jesus, the one who raises a person's sense of dignity and gives courage.

So I went, and for two weeks I toured the country, preaching in big assembly halls and stadiums and inviting people to follow Jesus the Lord, who sets people free from all bondage, including the political bondage. Thousands responded.[2] At the end of our mission I received a phone call from the minister of culture of the newly independent state of Lithuania inviting me to his office. Surprised by such an invitation I went, only to be caught by an even greater surprise. The minister urged me to go home and activate the Protestant community in Western Europe to help the government of Lithuania to set up a "Christian university." "We need to transform the mind of our people. And this can only be done by Christians who know and follow Jesus," he said. "I am an atheist," the minister continued, "but atheism has brought slavery to Lithuania. You preach in your sermons that Jesus offers truth, real morality, and dignity, and you say the only precondition is to understand what truth is. I agree, therefore come and teach my people the truth." The minister offered us all the political support needed for the establishment of a Lithuanian Christian university. "Such a university is a political necessity," he said, concluding his appeal.

It is a long story, but today the Lithuanian Christian College (LCC) International University in Klaipeda is, in every respect, a vital Christian witness and an important educational institution in a thriving nation that long ago became a member of the European Community.[3] Hundreds of graduates of LCC have become both devoted Christians and transforming agents in their nation, just as the minister had requested years before.

It was only years later I realized how political the act of establishing a Christian institution in Lithuania was. It has obviously added to democracy and meaningful societal development in a former Soviet space. I also realized the crucial role Christians played in dismantling the unjust Soviet system.[4] The power driving change was less in military weapons than in an alternative lifestyle, in the ability to live in dignity even when this meant losing every bit of it.

---

2. See the report of the tour in Johannes Reimer, *Ende einer Suppermacht* (Basel: Brunnen Verlag, 2009), 135–139.

3. See the story of the LCC in Sarah Klassen, ed., *Lithuania Christian College: A Work in Progress* (Winnipeg: Leona DeFehr, 2001). More about the university today in http://www.lcc. lt (Last access: 1 October 2015).

4. Reimer, *Am Ende einer Suppermacht*, 69–132.

1.3. Theological Perspectives Given

My personal experience led me to deepen my understanding through training. I am especially thankful to my theological teachers at the University of South Africa, namely David J. Bosch (1929–1992) and Willem A. Saayman (1942–2015) and the Mennonite theologian John Howard Yoder (1927–1997) who helped me in my search for a theology of political involvement.

It was Professor Saayman, long time South African missionary to Zambia and then professor of missiology at the University of South Africa, who clearly expressed for me a need to determine what a political mandate of the church encompasses. He pointed to the fact that mission is always involved in politics. In fact mission and politics, says Saayman, are interrelated.[5] A "pure ecclesiastical (also missionary) neutrality" does not exist.[6] Saayman agreed with the Dutch missiologist Johannes Verkuyl that the very confession of Israel "Yahweh is God" and of the church in the New Testament "Jesus is Lord" "has always been both a statement of faith and also a political credo which leads inescapably to political choices and tasks."[7] And he based his arguments on the one hand on John Howard Yoder's theology of the cross as the focal point of Jesus teaching.[8] For Yoder and consequently Saayman the cross was "the political, legally to be expected result of a moral clash with the powers ruling his society."[9] According to Yoder there is no way to divorce the teachings of Jesus from politics. His arguments have shaped my theology of mission.

On the other hand, Saayman correlates mission and politics because God's acts in human history to shape the social space according to his own will and his rule are just. God establishes justice, a genuine political dimension, in human history. He is always interested in the neighbour, in the other, and their condition. Saayman states: "Because of this very basic choice for the other, justice is so central to the church's mission – and binds it so firmly to the ordering of human society."[10] He goes so far as to claim, with a WCC statement, "Outside of justice there is no salvation."[11]

---

5. Willem Saayman, *Christian Mission in South Africa* (Pretoria: University of South Africa, 1991), 1–16.

6. Saayman, 11.

7. Saayman, 12. See Johannes Verkuyl, *Inleiding in de nieweste Zendingswetenschap* (Kampen: Kok, 1975), 534.

8. Saayman, 14.

9. John Howard Yoder, *The Politics of Jesus* (Grand Rapids: Eerdmans, 1972), 132.

10. Saayman, *Christian Mission*, 12.

11. Saayman, 12.

Saayman's conclusions and arguments intrigued and challenged me in my personal search for a biblically sound and at the same time practically reliable understanding of the correlation between mission and politics. He spoke as a missionary who cared deeply for evangelization of the ignorant godless and at the same time a biblical realist committed to God and his mission. Some of what I have learned from my beloved late professor is presented on the pages of this book.

1.4. Ecumenical Movement: A Red Flag

The concept of a *missio politica* was developed in the ecumenical movement. It is the International Missionary Council (IMC) – and later after the merger of the IMC with the World Council of Churches (WCC) in 1961 the Church's Commission on Internal Affairs (CCIA) of the WCC – that laid the theological foundations for what was then called a *missio politica ecumenica*.[12] The concept developed here encouraged churches worldwide to accept their political engagement as a vital part of their mission.[13] The Dutch missiologist Johannes Verkuyl expanded the concept and gave it a solid evangelical theological foundation.[14]

It is this background that raises red flags in evangelical circles as soon as the term *missio politica* is named. The WCC's political involvement was in so many ways problematic. The term was closely associated with a theology that bluntly identified well-being with salvation, disregarding eternal salvation as such, and identified the kingdom of God with a humanization project. In praxis, the WCC's support of liberation movements in Africa or Latin America by offering weapons, for instance, determined the split between conciliar and evangelical Christians.

There can be no question – I carried my red flag with me when arriving in South Africa to continue my studies under David J. Bosch and Willem A. Saayman. And there were many plausible reasons to do so. David Bosch did not argue against me. On contrary he even supported me in my critique and added many more valid insights to my critical views. He himself seemed also to carry his own red flag. But then he asked me one day a simple question which made me drop my flag forever. He said, "Johannes, what does God say about

---

12. See in this regard S. A. Teinonen, *Missio Politica Ecumenica* (Helsinki: Finnish Society of Missionary Research, 1961).

13. Teinonen, *Missio,* 10.

14. Verkuyl, *Inleiding.*

the injustice in the world? The Ecumenics might be wrong, he is not. Do not allow the wrong doers to determine your theology; let the Bible do this for you. Reject what is wrong; accept what is right; and never, never overgeneralize." Amazingly simple, as are many of the other insights David Bosch gave me. This is why I am prepared to learn from all people, as long as what they say is reflected in Scripture.

I understand how problematic terminology is. Especially when it comes to politics and the church. John R. W. Stott wrote years ago: "It is the use of the word 'political' which causes red warning lights to flash in the minds of many evangelicals. They have always engaged in humanitarian work, especially in medical and educational programs; it is political activity which they have often fought shy."[15]

Stott courageously worked through the problematic language and the problematic theologies behind it to come to his own view of a mission with a clear political dimension. His way is marked by the founding of the Lausanne Movement and the Lausanne Committee for World Evangelisation (LCWE), causing a deep split in world Christianity, but also by a growing force of Evangelicals for Social Justice (ESJ), who worked from an integral understanding of God's mission in the world. As with many other evangelicals, he became open to a more wholistic view on what the mission of God in the world encompassed.

It is my hope that this short essay encourages others to work their way through the Bible and clarify the issue for themselves. Especially those who are involved in mission must lay a solid foundation for their mission in the world. Without proper knowledge people might perish (Hos 4:6), but understanding the truth leads to freedom and proper action (John 8:32).

1.5. The Question at Stake

In our essay we will examine the theological validity of the political engagement of the church. Does the church of Christ have a political mandate? Is political engagement even a vital part of its mission? Or should the church as an institution distance itself from all politics and withdraw from an active participation in the life of the world, consciously accepting a purely religious role? Is such a role realistic?

---

15. John R. W. Stott et al, *New Issues Facing Christians Today* (Grand Rapids: Zondervan, 2006), 13.

These questions are not new. Christians in different times and contexts have attempted a solution. Some, for instance, the Orthodox,[16] the Roman Catholic,[17] and the mainline Protestant church[18] clearly accepted a political role. Others, however, the Anabaptist, for example, withdrew from any involvement[19] and became what is known as "the quiet in the land,"[20] blaming the others for having lost sight of the gospel.

Who is right? The political involvement of Christians still divides Christians all over the world in conformist and nonconformist parties. What is needed is a theological foundation, a biblical perspective on the issue, since the Bible is the ultimate guide for us Christians in all questions of our life and mission. What does the Bible say about our mission in the world? Are we politically responsible for society or not?

1.6. The Perspective Matters

The vast majority of Christians in the world understand mission as God's mission as they read the Bible.[21] He is the source and the prime agent of mission. Whoever defines the mission of the church will have to start with God and his plan and action for and in the world. The questions to ask are:

- What did God have in mind when creating the world and us humans?
- Where is he leading the world?
- What is our human destiny?
- What is God's great narrative, his big picture for the world?
- What is *his* mission?

---

16. See, as an example, *The Social Doctrine of the Russian Orthodox Church*. More in Charles C. West, "The Russian Orthodox Church and Social Doctrine: A Commentary on Fundamentals of the Social Conception of the Russian Orthodox Church," *Occasional Papers on Religion in Eastern Europe* 22, no. 2 (2002), Article 3. Online, http://digitalcommons.georgefox.edu/ree/vol22/iss2/3 (1.10.2015).

17. See, for instance, the "Compendium of the Social Doctrine of the Church," online, http://www.vatican.va/roman_curia/pontifical_councils/justpeace/documents/rc_pc_justpeace_doc_20060526_compendio-dott-soc_en.html (1.10.2015).

18. A case in point is the political role of American mainline churches. See Kraig Beyerlein and Mark Chaves, "The Political Activities of Religious Congregations in the United States," *Journal for the Scientific Study of Religion* 42, no. 2 (June 2003): 229–246.

19. James Urry, *Mennonites, Politics and Peoplehood: Europe-Russia-Canada*, 1525–1980 (Winnipeg: University of Manitoba Press, 2006).

20. Urry, *Mennonites*, 3.

21. There is a plethora of publications discussing the basic concept of *missio Dei*. See for instance Christopher Wright, *The Mission of God: Unlocking the Bible's Grand Narrative* (Downers Grove: IVP Academic, 2006).

It is the Bible and only the Bible that offers answers to such questions. It is God's great narrative that we are called to unlock in order to understand his mission in the world. Only his view on mission offers us a proper frame of reference for the mission of the church, and knowing the frame of reference, we might be able to look at the details. We seek, therefore, to read the Scriptures from a missiological perspective. Looking at the Bible from a more narrow view might mislead the reader and confuse rather than answer our question of political responsibility as Christians. Asking for an answer within a frame of God's divine will, however, sharpen our view on what he himself determines to be right or wrong.

2

God and His Mission in the Old Testament

2.1. God – the Source and Foundation

The Old Testament reveals to us God as the creator of the universe, the omnipresent and omnipotent self. Israel, God's people, is called to confess: "Hear, O Israel, the LORD our God is one LORD" (Deut 6:4). But God is not just *their* God, he is God of the whole earth (Gen 18:25; Ps 22:27–28; Jer 10:6–7; Dan 2:47). "All the Earth is mine" (Exod 19:5), says God. Nations are claiming their own gods (Exod 9:14; Deut 3:23; Ps 96:5), which in reality are not gods at all but rather man-made idols (Isa 37:19). Israel is commanded not to have other deities before Yahweh (Exod 20:3). The prophet Isaiah quotes God as saying: "For I am God and there is no other" (Isa 46:9).

The Old Testament perspective on God and gods is immensely important for a theology of mission. Why? First, it sets a pattern of authority. Whatever we humans say about life and the meaning of life on earth has to be referred back to the author of life: God, the only source of all being. This includes mission. There cannot be any other reason for mission except what God declares to be a valid reason. Mission must therefore be thought and argued theologically. It is first and foremost God's mission.

Second, it excludes other secondary sources and foundations for the meaning of life. The gods of humans are nothing and their religions are just a shadow of what is offered by Yahweh, the only true God. Mission will never draw on their insights, except those insights that conform to what God reveals to us in his Word.

The Old Testament concept of God offers to us the first correlativum for a biblical theology of mission – it connects mission to the very nature of God and describes mission as an action of the sovereign God. We will only properly answer our question of how mission relates to politics by finding out what the mission of God encompasses. And to do so we start where God's missionary story starts – in the Old Testament.

2.2. God Created the World with a Purpose

God reveals himself first as creator of the world. He created the world, according to the Old Testament, *ex nihilo,* out of nothing (Gen 1:1–2:3). There was no universe before him. He is the author of the world. The prophet Isaiah quotes Yahweh saying, "Heaven is my throne, and the earth is my footstool. Where is the house you will build for me? Where will my resting place be? Has not my hand made all these things, and so they came into being?" (Isa 66:1–2).[1]

God is the creator of the world, and whatever he creates has meaning. There is a divine plan in what God does. He followed a mission by creating the universe. The act of creation must therefore be viewed as an act of mission, indicating to us the second issue of a biblical theology of mission. Whoever wants to discuss God's mission in the world will have to begin with creation, the point where all mission practically started. God himself is the sending and the sent one. He is the source of his own mission. Mission is, therefore, first and foremost God's mission – *missio Dei.* God is the Lord of mission and the active missionary in one person. In his wisdom the world was created by him, and he created his world in order to fulfil his own plan. Creation and mission is the second correlativum the Old Testament presents to us. God, the missionary, starts his mission to the world by creating the world with a purpose in mind.

The Old Testament perspective on creation is important for a theology of mission. It names the frame of mission. God is not concerned with us humans only – he put a universe in motion. It is this universe he has created and will be concerned about through history. Mission must therefore always include all creation not just parts of it.

---

1. Compare Job 38:4–6; Ps 104:1–30.

2.3. Humans Are Set to Fulfill God's Plan

God created the world and placed in the midst of his creation man made in his own image (Gen 1:26). Adam and Eve, the first humans, were created to rule, multiply, and cultivate the Earth (Gen 1:28). They were made godlike and his mission was given into their hands (Gen 1:26). This mission is best described as a cultural mandate.[2] He created the world and humans will cultivate and transform the world into a place of godly living: cultivate land, build cities, develop music, and enjoy life (Gen 5).[3] God the ultimate missionary appoints men and women to realize his will in time and space.

And by doing so, he does not leave humans alone. His call starts with a blessing (Gen 1:28a). God's blessing and mission belong together. Whoever he sends he blesses beforehand. Even more, he becomes a covenant partner who assures his presence in everything the sent one may go through. See in this regard God's covenants with Noah (Gen 6:1–19), Abram (Gen 12:1–3), and others. Sending and blessing is the third correlativum of mission the Old Testament reveals to us.

2.4. God Reveals Himself in History

God creates and keeps the world running. The Old Testament bears great witness to God's salvific engagement in the world. From the first pages of Genesis to the last prophet of the Old Testament, we see a God who cares. The Old Testament does not spiritualize God's presence; his acts are real and relevant to the story of his people. God is a complete opposite of the idols of the nations. They appear spiritualized and of the occult; Yahweh instead reveals himself in acts of life, a God in the midst of people. His presence is perceivable. The Old Testament uses anthropomorphic language to express this. God walks in the garden (Gen 3:8), he talks to men and to the snake (Gen 3:14–15; Gen 4:6–16; 7:1–5; etc.).

People form their understanding of him by experience. He clearly seeks dialogue and fellowship with humans. Known as the God of Abraham, Isaac, and Jacob, he reveals his will to the chosen ones and works through them.

---

2. Roger E. Hedlund, *A Biblical Theology of the Mission of the Church in the World* (Grand Rapids, MI: Baker, 1985), 23.

3. Stuhlmueller names the process Akkulturation (D. Senior and C. Stuhlmueller, *The Biblical Foundations of Mission* [Maryknoll, NY: Orbis, 1983], 36ff).

Whoever attempts to understand God's missionary heart will have to search for him in history. God's mission happens in time and space; it takes place in the world. He reveals himself in the midst of real life, and there are no parts of life he is not interested in. He constitutes nations, for example, he establishes Israel in a land of promise (Gen 15:1–18) and then leads the nation out of bondage in Egypt (Exodus). With great detail and interest in life, he offers Israel laws covering their social, economic, political, and spiritual life (Leviticus). Wherever God appears among his people, life is enriched. Wherever God speaks, life is at stake. For our theology of mission we will have to postulate a fourth correlativum of revelation and history, mission and context.

2.5. God Seeks to Heal His Creation

God created men with a free will, and our forefathers decided to disobey him, turning our human history into one of sin and sorrow (Gen 3–6). The result is the loss of eternal life, and death enters human history. But God does not destroy humans totally. He reveals his mercy and love instead.

The authors of the Old Testament underline both: the human dilemma of sin on the one hand and God's repeated acts of redemption on the other. In fact, the issue of redemption seems to run through all Old Testament books. God sanctions human sin, but he does not remove his blessing and caring hand from his creation. He sends a flood to destroy, but he also establishes his covenant with Noah (Gen 6). He disperses the nations, but then he elects Abram to become a blessing for all nations (Gen 11–12; Gen 12:3), and from the nations he elects Israel to become a blessing for the nations of the world.[4] The aim of all missionary energy flowing from God's heart seems to culminate in the "salvation for all people" (Isa 49:6). Whoever attempts a biblical theology of mission will have to reflect God's redemptive heart. Redemption and restoration are central issues in the Old Testament. A fifth correlativum – that of mission and restoration, mission and redemption – must be dealt with in laying a foundation for missions from the Old Testament. "Man's tragic alienation from God and fellow-man is the fact behind the Christian mission."[5]

---

4. See the arguments of Stuhlmueller in Senior, *The Biblical Foundation*, 13.
5. Hedlund, *A Biblical Theology*, 24.

2.6. Israel – Example and Paradigm

The Old Testament is largely a book about Israel. God created Israel to demonstrate his will to the nations of the world. In Deuteronomy 28:9–10 we read: "The LORD will establish you as his holy people, as he promised you on oath, if you keep the commands of the LORD your God and walk in his ways. Then all the peoples on earth will see that you are called by the name of the LORD, and they will fear you."

Israel is there because God is concerned with the nations. Samuel and Sugden rightly underline the special calling of Israel to be the light for the nations (see, for instance, Gen 17:6; Isa 42:6; 49:6), a model of a nation according to God's will and heart.[6] Israel's destiny is in many ways predesigned as God's missionary paradigm for the world. Whoever attempts to formulate a biblical theology of mission will have to examine the nature, the structure, and the laws by which the Israelite community was to function. God's will for his nation has immediate implications for his will for the nations. Being a blessing to the nations implies knowing what a blessed life contains. A theology of mission will have to examine the sixth correlativum of mission and Israel's role in the midst of the nations.

2.7. A Holy Nation among the Nations

The Old Testament focuses on Israel, God's chosen people. But the story of Israel is told in constant relation to the nations around it. In fact the stage on which the story of God's people unfolds is built by nations around and in Israel. Even the most constitutive event in Israel's history, the exodus from Egypt, is accompanied by crowds of "other people" (Exod 12:38). Those "others" have always been around (Num 11:4) and they become both a constant challenge and a divine call to Israel. They challenge Israel's belief system, introduce idolatry and immoral behaviour to Israel, and at the same time learn how God molds and saves his nation. Israel is God's example for the nations. Consequently, the prophets see an eschatological gathering of the nations in Jerusalem (Isa 2:2–4).[7] In Jerusalem, God establishes his throne to rule his new creation (Isa 35:1–19; Isa 65:17–18). Zion is the place where God lives (Ps 24:7–10). The nations of the world will gather at Zion (Isa 11:10), and here they will learn

---

6. Vinney Samuel and Chris Sugden, *Church in Response to Human Need* (Oxford: Regnum, 1987), 128.

7. See also Micah 4:1–5; Ps 36:8–9; Ps 50:2, etc.

his ways of life (Isa 2:2–4) and adore him (Ps 22:27–31). At Zion the nations of the world will return to God (Zech 2:11), God himself bringing the nations to Zion (Isa 56:7–8).

Does the Old Testament teach a proactive mission of Israel to the nations? A number of scholars support such an idea.[8] Proponents of an active role of Israel in God's mission usually point to the book of Jonah to establish their arguments.[9] In their perception the sending of a prophet of Israel to a Gentile nation is evidence enough of God's missionary mandate to Israel. Others disagree.[10] There is no question that the book of Jonah clearly states God's claim to rule all nations. Nineveh is also his city (4:11). And he cares for the people of Nineveh. Jonah, an Israelite, is sent to warn them, but God's divine commission runs against Jonah's convictions. He is not ready to follow God's command but is forced to do so anyway. The text does not say more. No reflection on any mission of Israel is given. Jonah is individually sent, as was Daniel or Esther. I can't see how this text establishes a call for Israel to go and preach to the nations.

Similarly problematic is the use of Zion-Psalms for justification of an active missionary role for Israel. Legrand[11] and Köstenberger[12] point us to the fact that Psalms are first of all liturgical songs of praise by Israel to the God of their salvation. Zion-Psalms are in no way different. They praise God who rules as king in Zion (Ps 47:93, 96–97, 99) in all his glory (Ps 5:7; 11:4; 65:4; 68:5; etc). The nations of the world are invited to come and participate in the blessings of Israel (72:8–11; 102:12–22). Nowhere is Israel called to go actively to the nations, the opposite is expected – the nations may come to Zion.

---

8. See, for instance, J. Bright, *The Kingdom of God in Bible and Church* (London: Lutterworth, 1955); Richard Schultz, "Und sie verkündigen meine Herrlichkeit unter den Nationen. Mission im Alten Testament unter besonderer Berücksichtigung von Jesaja," in *Werdet meine Zeugen*, trans. by Hans Kasdorf and Friedemann Walldorf (Neuhausen-Stuttgart: Hänssler, 1996), 33–53; Walter Kaiser, *Mission in the Old Testament: Israel as Light to the Nations* (Grand Rapids, MI: Baker, 2000); Charles H. Scobbie, "Israel and the Nations: An Essay in Biblical Theology," *Tyndale Bulletin* 43, no. 2 (1992): 283–305.

9. Bright, *The Kingdom of God,* 162–163; Ian M. Hay, *Isaiah and the Great Commission: An Old Testament Study of New Testament Missions* (Charlotte, NC: SIM, 1994), 22ff; Kaiser, *Mission in the Old Testament,* 65–71; etc.

10. See the discussion in Andreas J. Köstenberger and Peter T. O'Brien, *Salvation to the End of the Earth: A Biblical Theology of Mission* (Downers Grove, IL: InterVarsity Press, 2001), 44f.

11. L. Legrand, *Unity and Plurality: Mission in the Bible* (Maryknoll, NY: Orbis, 2002), 8.

12. Köstenberger, *Salvation to the End,* 50.

The third source of a possible active mission of Israel is found in the four Ebed Yahweh songs in the book of the prophet Isaiah[13] (42:1–4; 49:1–6; 50:4–9; 52:13–53:12; see also 61:1–3). The servant of God is presented as God's chosen (42:1), sent to speak and teach law and justice to the nations (42:4–6), a law established by God, the creator of the world (Isa 40:14–27). He and only he decides about right or wrong in the universe.[14] The servant will teach God's law to the nations (49:1). And Israel with him (49:6). The prophet even calls him Israel (49:3). He will restore Israel (49:5–6) and proclaim salvation to the ends of the Earth (49:6b). Some interpreters see in the naming of servant "Israel" an indicator for a collective figure and therefore a missionary call to the whole of Israel.[15] I can't share such an interpretation. The servant is called to restore and bring Israel back to Zion (49:8–13). Israel is blind (42:18–22), misunderstands and mocks the servant (53:3f). In fact he takes the sin of Israel on him (53:8ff). As a result of his work, Israel is restored (54–55) and the nations gather on Zion.

Köstenberger and O'Brien conclude their investigation with the following summary: "To contend that Israel had a missionary task and should have engaged in mission as we understand it today, goes beyond the evidence. There is no suggestion in the Old Testament that Israel should have engaged in 'cross cultural and foreign mission.'"[16]

The Old Testament nowhere teaches a proactive mission of Israel to the nations. Israel is called to be a holy nation among nations, a priestly mediator (Zech 8:20–23), but never a proactive missionary. This does not mean Israel has *no* mission. The opposite is true. Israel's role in world history is to model a nation obedient to God. They are given the commandments of the Lord (Exod 20). They know what is right and wrong in the sight of God. Israel is given a godly social and economic order. The order of the *Jobelyear* (Lev 25) presents a paradigm of living that contains both justice and prosperity. It is obvious, as Paul House rightly underlines, that a *Jobel* culture required a functioning relationship between Israel and Yahweh.[17] The fear of God (Lev 25:17), relying on God's provision (Lev 25:18–22), leaving the land in God's hand (Lev 25:23–

---

13. See Hedlund, *A Biblical Theology*, 110–119; Scobbie, *Israel*, 291–292; D. F. Payne, "The Meaning of Mission in Isaiah 40–55," in *Mission and Meaning: Essays Presented to Peter Cotterell*, eds. T. Lane Billington and M. Turner (Carlisle: Paternoster, 1995), 3–11.

14. Köstenberger, *Salvation to the End*, 46.

15. See for instance Kaiser, *Mission in the Old Testament*, 63.

16. Köstenberger, *Salvation to End*, 35.

17. Paul R. House, *Old Testament Theology* (Downers Grove: IVP Academic, 1998), 147.

24) and identifying itself as belonging to the Lord (Lev 35–55) is defining a frame of reference for such a culture.[18] Yes, Israel has a mission, a distinct mission. In the words of Chris Wright ". . . Israel had a missional role in the midst of the nations – implying that they had an identity and role connected to God's ultimate intention of blessing the nations."[19] In 1937 the missiologist Bengt Sunkler introduced the idea of centripetal vs centrifugal mission.[20] The mission of Israel is centripetal, it draws the nations to come and see the glory of God at Zion. A centrifugal mission as described by the Great Commission of Jesus commissions the disciples to go the nations (Matt 28:19–20). There is no evidence of a centrifugal mission in the Old Testament.[21]

A theology of mission must address the universal nature of God's rule. The correlation of Israel and the nations, God's people and peoples of the world, and even more so, God and the nations, must be addressed as one of the central notions of the Old Testament.

2.8. The Messiah Comes from Israel

The realization of God's redemptive plan lies in the hands of an eschatological Messiah, who restores both Israel and the nations (Isa 61:1–2).

For a theology of mission the extraordinary role of Ebed Yahweh, the suffering servant of God, must be discussed. He is believed to be the Messiah of Israel and ultimately the Messiah of the nations. The seventh correlation of God's mission and his Messiah is crucial to both the destiny of Israel and, at the same time, the nations – the world as whole. It is this promise that Jesus and his disciples referred to, establishing their redemptive mission to the world (for instance, Luke 4:18, from Isa 61:1–2, and Acts 2).

The Old Testament lays foundations and formulates a frame of reference for a theology and praxis of mission in which all the main elements of God's mission are presented. It names and frames a world in which God and his very being are understood, and God's idea of humanity is exorcised, and those

---

18. House.

19. Christopher J. H. Wright, *The Mission of God: Unlocking the Bible's Great Narrative* (Downers Grove, IL: InterVarsity Press, 2006), 24–25.

20. Bengt Sundkler, "Jésus et les païens," in *Contributions à l'étude de la pensée missionaire dans le Nouveau Testament*, Arbeiten und Mitteilungen aus dem neutestamentlichen Seminar zu Uppsala VI, (Uppsala, Sweden: Neutestentliches Seminar zu Uppsala, 1937), 1–38.

21. Johannes Blauw, *The Missionary Nature of the Church: A Survey of Biblical Theology of Mission* (New York, NY: McGraw-Hill, 1962), 35; Craig Ott, Stephen J. Strauss, Timothy C. Tennent, *Encountering Theology of Mission* (Grand Rapids, MI: Baker, 2010), 23.

destructive forces which divide men from God and isolates humans from God's divine blessing are pointed out. With Israel God establishes a living example and marks the issues involved. George W. Peters finds a way to summarize the validity of the Old Testament for a missionary theology. He writes, "The Old Testament does not contain mission; it is itself 'missions' in the world."[22]

It is wrong to read any proactive mission of Israel into the Old Testament,[23] but the mission of the church to the nations as described by the New Testament is only properly understood against the salvation-historical background of the Old Testament. The German missiologist Hans-Werner Gensichen rightly states: "Even when the Old Testament knows nothing about an active mission of God's people in a sense of going to the nations, it defines the salvation-historical frame in which such mission is made possible. God's mission to the nations in the Old Testament is a promise, depicted in Israel's story, and is waiting for its fulfillment in Christ."[24]

---

22. George W. Peters, *A Biblical Theology of Mission* (Chicago, IL: Moody, 1972), 29.

23. See also the universalistic texts in Gen 12:1–3; Amos 9; Ps 72:8–19; Isa 2:2–5; Mic 4:1–5; Isa 40; Mal 1:11. But all these passages do not constitute a proactive sending of Israel to the nations. See Hans-Werner Gensichen, *Glaube für die Welt: Theologische Aspekte der Mission* (Gütersloh: Mohn, 1971), 62.

24. Gensichen, *Glaube für die Welt*, 62.

3

Mission and Politics in the Old Testament

3.1. Creation and the Cultural Mandate

We have searched the Old Testament for its understanding of mission, establishing a number of crucial *correlativa* for a possible interrelationship between mission and politics. Does the Old Testament correlate the two terms? And if so – how? Let's examine the main postulates by starting with creation.

God's story with the world starts with creation. In Genesis 1:1–12 we read:

> In the beginning God created the heavens and the earth. Now the earth was formless and empty, darkness was over the surface of the deep, and the Spirit of God was hovering over the waters.
>
> And God said, "Let there be light," and there was light. God saw that the light was good, and he separated the light from the darkness. God called the light "day" and the darkness he called "night." And there was evening, and there was morning – the first day.
>
> And God said, "Let there be an expanse between the waters to separate water from water." So God made the expanse and separated the water under the vault from the water above it. And it was so. God called the expanse "sky." And there was evening, and there was morning – the second day.
>
> And God said, "Let the water under the sky be gathered to one place, and let dry ground appear." And it was so. God called the dry ground "land," and the gathered waters he called "seas." And God saw that it was good.

> Then God said, "Let the land produce vegetation: seed-bearing plants and trees on the land that bear fruit with seed in it, according to their various kinds." And it was so. The land produced vegetation: plants bearing seed according to their kinds and trees bearing fruit with seed in it according to their kinds. And God saw that it was good.

It is easy to see – God created the world with a purpose. There is a mandate behind his work. Whatever he does follows a mission. There can be no being in God's creation without a meaning and purpose. God the creator is a missionary God.

And into this wonderfully and perfectly created world God placed humans. In Genesis 1:27–31 we read:

> So God created mankind in his own image, in the image of God he created them; male and female he created them.
>
> God blessed them and said to them, "Be fruitful and increase in number; fill the earth and subdue it. Rule over the fish in the sea and the birds in the sky and over every living creature that moves on the ground."
>
> Then God said, "I give you every seed-bearing plant on the face of the whole earth and every tree that has fruit with seed in it. They will be yours for food. And to all the beasts of the earth and all the birds in the sky and all the creatures that move along the ground – everything that has the breath of life in it – I give every green plant for food." And it was so.
>
> God saw all that he had made, and it was very good.

Again, the text allows no other interpretation – humankind has been created for a purpose. Humans are set to cultivate and rule the created world in accordance with God's will. God gives us what we may call a cultural mandate.[1] Our human mission is to order, civilize, and rule the world. In other words – humans are responsible to determine a meaningful space for living, a "way of Life," "strategies for living."[2] The American missiologist George W. Peters states:

---

1. For more dicussion on the cultural mandate see, for instance George W. Peters, *A Biblical Theology*, 166–170; Edward C. Pentecost, *Issues in Missiology: An Introduction* (Grand Rapids: Baker, 1982), 37–42.

2. See in this regard definitions of what culture is in Lothar Käser, *Fremde Kulturen: Eine Einführung in die Ethnologie* (Bad Liebenzell: VLM, 1997), 37.

The . . . mandate was spoken to Adam as representative of the race and involves the whole realm of human culture . . . It includes the natural and social aspects of man such as habitat, agriculture, industrialization, commerce, politics, social and moral order, academic and scientific advancement, health, education, and physical care . . . such culture was to benefit man and glorify God.[3]

This is, in other words, a political mandate. Humans are called to govern the world, and this is where all human reflection on God's mission in the world begins.[4] His mission is political by nature. Humans are called to join him in governing the world, and "government is the regulation of public affairs, and politics is the means by which people determine whose views of government will prevail."[5] The term politics comes from the Greek *politicos* and describes a way to relate to a socio-cultural space.[6] John Stott properly defines politics as "the art of living together in community,"[7] or Willem A. Saayman, who understand politics, defines it as "practice and art of government of human affairs in relation to the whole of life."[8]

In conclusion: God's first mandate for humankind is political in nature, and this mandate has never been taken back from humans, not even after the fall of man in the garden of Eden. There is no space for humans to withdraw from political responsibility. Human life on earth is political because God has honoured humans to govern the world he made.

3.2. Blessed to Be a Blessing for the Nations

The great plan of God to establish his reign on earth by calling humans to become his managers of all creation ended in disaster. Instead of following God's command, the first humans were disobedient, which allowed sin to take over, and soon wrongdoing covered the earth (Gen 3–6). We know our human story as told to us in the Bible. But we also know God's great plan to save the human race from self-destruction.

---

3. Peters, *A Biblical Theology*, 166.

4. Köstenberger, *Salvation to the Ends of the Earth*, 25.

5. https://www.tkc.edu/academics/what-is-politics/ (Last access: 23 August 2017).

6. See, for instance, Henry George Liddell, Robert Scott, πολιτικός "A Greek-English Lexicon." Perseus Digital Library in: http://www.perseus.tufts.edu/hopper/text?doc=Perseus %3Atext%3A1999.04.0057%3Aentry%3Dpolitiko%2Fs (Last access: 23 August 2017).

7. Stott, *New Issues*, 14.

8. Saayman, *Christian Mission*, 5.

His salvific plan begins with his covenant with Noah (Gen 9:8–11), and in this covenant God renews the cultural mandate to Noah and his sons as well as all descendants after them. Then God calls Abraham to leave his nation in order to become a new nation in the midst of all other nations. God blesses him to become a blessing for all the peoples of the world (Gen 12:3). Lesslie Newbigin is right when he states, "Those who are chosen to be bearers of blessing are chosen for the sake of *all*. The covenant of Noah is revoked. The promised blessing is, in the end, for all the nations."[9]

Israel is established and becomes the battlefield for God's idea of a nation according to his heart. The history of this chosen nation marks the Old Testament. It is a history of failure, sin, delivery, and forgiveness: a difficult and yet – time after time – a renewed relationship of God to his people. After all, they are to be a blessing to all nations. Waldron Scott rightly underlines the fact that "God's gracious purpose for all mankind permeates the entire Old Testament."[10] David says "all ends of the earth shall remember and turn to the LORD; and all the families of nations will bow down before him" (Ps 22:27). The prophets Isaiah (25:6–7) and Joel (3:28) clearly see the nations of the Lord one day turning to the knowledge of the Lord and worshiping him alone. God blesses Israel to bless the nations that they may see the Lord and worship him in truth.

Israel is God's prime chosen witness. God is, therefore, concerned with the right worship of Israel, and this worship is literally permeated by social issues. The Israelites were more than surprised to hear at the height of their religious development the words of their prophet Isaiah, who claimed God's unwillingness to bless them because their attitude towards the weak and the needy was unjust. In Isaiah 58:1–14 we read:

> Shout it aloud, do not hold back. Raise your voice like a trumpet. Declare to my people their rebellion and to the descendants of Jacob their sins. For day after day they seek me out; they seem eager to know my ways, as if they were a nation that does what is right and has not forsaken the commands of its God. They ask me for just decisions and seem eager for God to come near them. "Why have we fasted," they say, "and you have not seen it? Why have we humbled ourselves, and you have not noticed?"

9. Lesslie Newbigin, *The Open Secret* (Grand Rapids: Eerdmans, 1978), 34; see also Waldron Scott, *Bring Forth Justice* (Grand Rapids: Eerdmans, 1980), 47.

10. Scott, *Bring Forth*, 47.

Yet on the day of your fasting, you do as you please and exploit all your workers. Your fasting ends in quarrelling and strife, and in striking each other with wicked fists. You cannot fast as you do today and expect your voice to be heard on high. Is this the kind of fast I have chosen, only a day for people to humble themselves? Is it only for bowing one's head like a reed and for lying in sackcloth and ashes? Is that what you call a fast, a day acceptable to the LORD?

Is not this the kind of fasting I have chosen: to lose the chains of injustice and untie the cords of the yoke, to set the oppressed free and break every yoke? Is it not to share your food with the hungry and to provide the poor wanderer with shelter – when you see the naked, to clothe them, and not to turn away from your own flesh and blood? Then your light will break forth like the dawn, and your healing will quickly appear; then your righteousness will go before you, and the glory of the LORD will be your rear guard. Then you will call, and the LORD will answer; you will cry for help, and he will say: Here am I.

If you do away with the yoke of oppression, with the pointing finger and malicious talk, and if you spend yourselves in behalf of the hungry and satisfy the needs of the oppressed, then your light will rise in the darkness, and your night will become like the noonday. The LORD will guide you always; he will satisfy your needs in a sun-scorched land and will strengthen your frame. You will be like a well-watered garden, like a spring whose waters never fail. Your people will rebuild the ancient ruins and will raise up the age-old foundations; you will be called Repairer of Broken Walls, Restorer of Streets with Dwellings.

If you keep your feet from breaking the Sabbath and from doing as you please on my holy day, if you call the Sabbath a delight and the LORD's holy day honourable, and if you honour it by not going your own way and not doing as you please or speaking idle words, then you will find your joy in the LORD, and I will cause you to ride in triumph on the heights of the land and to feast on the inheritance of your father Jacob. The mouth of the LORD has spoken.

Right worship and right living are clearly interrelated in God's way of life. About Abraham God says, ". . . for I have chosen him that he may direct his children and his household after him to keep the way of the Lord by doing what and just" (Gen 18:19). Justice and righteousness are what determine the culture of God's chosen people and not religious rituals only. The two words are often used together in order to describe what we call today social justice.[11] God is calling people to become a blessing to the nations, and his blessing will be determined by a just and righteous society and culture. Where he reigns "justice [will] roll down like a river, and righteousness like an ever-flowing stream" (Amos 5:24). In fact social justice reflects the very character of God. "He loves righteousness and justice (Ps 33:5; see also Ps 37:28). He is the mighty king, lover of justice (Ps 99:4) who prefers righteousness and justice to sacrifice (Prov 21:3).

Abraham is commissioned to see that his children keep the way of the Lord by doing justice and righteousness. To live according to God's commands means to live in social justice. This is what Israel is reminded throughout her entire history. God frees his people from slavery in Egypt and then reminds them: "You shall not wrong a stranger or oppress him, for you were strangers in the land of Egypt. You shall not afflict any widow or orphan. If you do afflict them and they cry out to me, I will surely hear their cry" (Exod 22:21–23). As the children of Israel move into Canaan, the land of promise, Moses declares: "Follow justice and justice alone, that you may live and possess the land which the LORD your God is giving you" (Deut 16:20).

The kings of Israel are later praised for being just, for instance, David is praised because he "did what was right and just . . . for all his people" (2 Sam 8:15) and his son Solomon is praised for his wisdom "because they saw that he had the wisdom of God to administer justice" (1 Kgs 3:28). Time and time again the children of Israel are called "to seek justice, correct oppression, defend the fatherless, plead for the widow" (Isa 1:16–17). In God's world, there can be no injustice. The prophet Isaiah paints an amazing picture of a future under God's rule. In Isaiah 16:4–5 (RSV) he states: "When the oppressor is no more, and destruction has ceased, and he who tramples under foot has vanished from the land, then a throne will be established in steadfast love, and on it will sit in faithfulness in the tent of David one who judges and seeks justice and is swift to do righteousness."

And this reign of the righteous is not just for Israel. The prophet continues: "Listen to me my people, and give ear to me my nation; for a law will go forth from me, and my justice for a light to the peoples. My deliverance draws near

---

11. See the arguments in Scott, *Bring Forth*, 49.

speedily, my salvation is gone forth, and my arms will rule the peoples; the coastlands wait for me, and for my arm they hope" (Isa 51:4–5 RSV).

In summary: God is a God of social justice. Where he reigns, there is no room for injustice and oppression. Whoever he calls and blesses to carry out his mission will be involved in social justice, in other words, in political action towards a better world.

3.3. The God Who Saves and Restores

The Old Testament presents to us the story of a nation among nations governed by people commissioned to live according to God's will in righteousness and justice. This story is foretold with all its ups and downs. God's people fall into the sin of disobedience, act unjustly and cause the righteous God to punish them. In this story God is the sovereign ruler, never compromising his sense for justice, but on the other hand, saving and restoring his sometimes stubborn people. Two major narratives become a kind of matrix for his rule: the exodus story for salvation and the Jubilee commandment for restoration.

In the exodus story God saves the Israelites from slavery in Egypt. It is, in all regards, a political action. Israel is enslaved, lives in bondage in Egypt, and is severely oppressed. God hears their cry and calls Moses to become the leader of Israel's liberation. The liberation of Israel is not only salvation from bondage, but they are also given for a task. Israel is saved from being a slave to becoming a chosen servant of God. God speaks to Moses:

> Thus you shall say to the house of Jacob, and tell the people of Israel: You have seen what I did to the Egyptians, and how I bore you on eagle's wings and brought you to myself. Now, therefore, if you will obey my voice and keep my covenant, you shall be my own possession among all peoples; for all the earth is mine, and you shall be to me a kingdom of priests and a holy nation. (Exod 19:3–6 RSV)

In other words, Israel's calling is to be God's people in the world, to model an alternative culture and lifestyle, a just nation, glorifying God, the creator of all. The prophet Isaiah comments on the spirituality of Israel and says: "Is not this the fast that I choose: to loose the bonds of wickedness, to undo the thongs of the yoke, to let the oppressed go free and to brake every yoke" (Isa 58:6 RSV). God has broken the chains of Israel's slavery in order to present to the world a people living by a different kind of social governance, a different kind of politics.

The best expression of this alternative justice and righteousness driven culture is the installation of the so-called Jubilee year in Leviticus 25. God commanded Moses:

> Speak to the Israelites and say to them: "When you enter the land I am going to give you, the land itself must observe a Sabbath to the LORD. For six years sow your fields, and for six years prune your vineyards and gather their crops. But in the seventh year the land is to have a year of Sabbath rest, a Sabbath to the LORD. Do not sow your fields or prune your vineyards. Do not reap what grows of itself or harvest the grapes of your untended vines. The land is to have a year of rest. Whatever the land yields during the Sabbath year will be food for you – for yourself, your male and female servants, and the hired worker and temporary resident who live among you, as well as for your livestock and the wild animals in your land. Whatever the land produces may be eaten.
>
> Count off seven Sabbath years – seven times seven years – so that the seven Sabbath years amount to a period of forty-nine years. Then have the trumpet sounded everywhere on the tenth day of the seventh month; on the Day of Atonement sound the trumpet throughout your land. Consecrate the fiftieth year and proclaim liberty throughout the land to all its inhabitants. It shall be a jubilee for you; each of you is to return to your family property and to your own clan. The fiftieth year shall be a jubilee for you; do not sow and do not reap what grows of itself or harvest the untended vines. For it is a jubilee and is to be holy for you; eat only what is taken directly from the fields.
>
> In this Year of Jubilee everyone is to return to their own property." (Lev 25:2–13)

The year of Jubilee was meant to be a kind of corrective, regulating the economy and society of Israel. Every fifty years land was to go back to its original owner without any reimbursement, for the land in Israel actually belonged to God, the Lord. Men were considered stewards, no more. The society of Israel was to go through a fifty year period of complete renewal as a vital part of God's covenant with his chosen people. This allowed for the breaking of any tradition of unjust distribution of power and wealth in the nation. The praxis of justice is, as Jose Miguez Bonino rightly claims, ". . . not a mere interpersonal relationship or social virtue; it is the very nature of the covenant with the Lord who practices justice."[12]

In this light the prophet Isaiah pronounces the word of the Lord by saying: "The law will go out from me, and my justice will become a light to the nations" (Isa 51:4). Israel, the chosen and obedient nation, living an authentic lifestyle, would become a place where God is seen and his glory displayed so the nations will come and worship him at Zion (Isa 66:19). A state properly run becomes a witness to God's glory and a point of interest to the nations of the world. This is, of course, highly political.

In summary: God's covenant with his people includes just living. In fact, he saves his people to become a model of a nation under his rule, a witness of his glory to the nations. The centripetal mission of Israel is highly political. The American scholar George Eldon Ladd summarizes: "The Old Testament nowhere holds forth the hope of a bodiless, nonmaterial, purely spiritual redemption . . ."[13] On the contrary salvation and redemption is in principle embodied in the everyday life of a nation.

3.4. Mission to All Nations

The God of justice has the world in mind. All nations, all creatures are subject of his concern. A man is blessed to bless nations. A nation is chosen to shine God's glory in the midst of the nations. God's mission is universal, and it aims to establish God's reign among the nations. The nations will be attracted by what they see in Israel. Israel's social order and culture becomes the most important indicator for Yahweh being God of Israel. In Isaiah 2:2–3 (RSV) we read:

> It shall come to pass in the latter days that the mountain of the House of the Lord shall be established as the highest of the mountains, and shall be raised above the hills; and all the nations shall flow to it and many peoples shall come and say: "Come let us go up to the mountain of the LORD, to the house of God of Jacob, that he may teach us his ways and that we may walk in his paths."

Similarly the prophet Zechariah has a vision. He writes:

> Many peoples and strong nations shall come to seek the LORD of hosts in Jerusalem, and entreat the favour of the Lord. Thus

---

12. Jose Miguez Bonino, *Christians and Marxists* (Grand Rapids: Eerdmans, 1976), 35.
13. George Eldon Ladd, *Jesus and the Kingdom* (New York, NY: Harper & Row, 1964), 72.

says the LORD of hosts: "In those days ten men from the nations of every tongue shall take hold of the robe of a Jew, saying, 'Let us go with you, for we have heard that God is with you.'" (Zech 8:22–23 RSV)

The glory of God is established in Israel's culture and society. Is this political? What else could it be? The model attracting the nations is lived out in concrete life and this is by all means political.

In summary: God's universal mission reaches to all nations. It aims to transform all life of the nations and has, therefore, clearly political implications.

3.5. The Messiah of Israel

Israel proves unable to fulfil God's divine mission assigned to her. Instead of becoming the point of divine attraction to the nations, the chosen nation is in deep need of liberation. Israel needs a Messiah. And God promises to send his chosen servant to save the nation and with the nation the world. Is his mission political? The prophet Isaiah receives a word from God portraying the Messiah that is to come. Isaiah 61:1–9 reads:

The Spirit of the Sovereign LORD is on me, because the LORD has anointed me to proclaim good news to the poor. He has sent me to bind up the broken-hearted, to proclaim freedom for the captives and release from darkness for the prisoners, to proclaim the year of the LORD's favour and the day of vengeance of our God, to comfort all who mourn, and provide for those who grieve in Zion – to bestow on them a crown of beauty instead of ashes, the oil of joy instead of mourning, and a garment of praise instead of a spirit of despair. They will be called oaks of righteousness, a planting of the LORD for the display of his splendour.

They will rebuild the ancient ruins and restore the places long devastated; they will renew the ruined cities that have been devastated for generations. Strangers will shepherd your flocks; foreigners will work your fields and vineyards. And you will be called priests of the LORD, you will be named ministers of our God. You will feed on the wealth of nations, and in their riches you will boast.

Instead of your shame you will receive a double portion, and instead of disgrace you will rejoice in your inheritance. And so you will inherit a double portion in your land, and everlasting joy will be yours.

"For I, the Lord, love justice; I hate robbery and wrongdoing. In my faithfulness I will reward my people and make an everlasting covenant with them. Their descendants will be known among the nations and their offspring among the peoples. All who see them will acknowledge that they are a people the LORD has blessed."

The Messiah as promised here is an eschatological figure coming to restore Israel in the spirit of Jubilee. And Jubilee is, as seen above, a highly political event.

In summary: The Messiah promised to Israel will come and restore the nation of Israel in the spirit of Jubilee. The restoration encompasses the whole of life and is obviously a political event.

3.6. The Mission of God and Politics in the Old Testament

Reading the biblical narrative on the mission of God in the Old Testament the conclusion seems clear. God's action in the world is all about creating and empowering life on earth. And wherever life is endangered, God sets out to liberate humans for life. It makes sense therefore to define mission as an "attempt to embody God's liberating presence in every human situation."[14] Participating in God's mission means consequently *"participating in God's liberating activity in the world."*[15]

God creates life and liberates life, however not without a purpose. He puts his own plan forward, and he works towards the establishment of his kingdom. The conditions of life in his kingdom are clearly pictured in the concept of Jubilee. Mission of God means, therefore, *human liberation in the light of the Jubilee.*[16] And this means it is justice-centred, involving all spheres of life, even economy and ecology.

The denial of the political dimension of God's mission in the Old Testament by saying that mission must be purely spiritual and apolitical is a sin. "It is the sin of apathy and slothfulness and consists of not caring, not deciding, not

---

14. J. N. J. Kritzinger, "Black Theology: Challenge to Mission," Unpublished DTh thesis (Pretoria, SA: Unisa, 1988), 6.

15. Saayman, *Christian Mission*, 7.

16. Saayman.

taking responsibility for the other and of avoiding the issue by saying that it is not my business."[17]

---

17. Saayman, *Christian Mission*, 13 quoting A. Nolan, *God in South Africa: The Challenge of the Gospel* (Cape Town: David Philip, 1988), 41.

4

Mission in the New Testament

4.1. The God of the New Testament

We have established an Old Testament view on mission and its interrelatedness with politics. The church of Christ relies, however, on the New Testament for its definitive position on biblical issues. This does not exclude the Old Testament, but it seeks a New Testament perspective on issues of life and mission. We do well, therefore, to examine what the New Testament teaches on mission in general and on the mission of the church in particular. We start with the same notion – which fixed our point of departure for our short journey through the Old Testament – with God. He is the initiator of mission in the New Testament. But unlike the Old Testament, God is presented to us in the New Testament as a triune God – Father, Son, and Holy Spirit. Whoever attempts to understand God's mission will, therefore, first have to explain the nature of the triune God and relate this theology to the Old Testament.

What does the New Testament teach us about God? Jesus the Messiah teaches us God as the Father, and he understands himself as God's Son. Leaving the earth he promised to send his Spirit, the Lord of mission (2 Cor 3:17). To speak about the mission of God in the New Testament means, therefore, to explore God in his Trinity.[1] Mission is central to the theology of the New Testament,[2] and as such, it is Trinitarian in nature. The German theologian Hahn speaks about the "implicit Trinitarian structure of the new-testamentarian

---

1. Tom Wright, *Bringing the Church to the World* (Minneapolis: Bethany House, 1992), 201.

2. Howard I. Marshall, *New Testament Theology* (Downers Grove: InterVarsity Press, 2004), 36; Wright, *The Mission of God*, 50; etc.

witness."[3] The mission of God in the world takes place in the name of the Father, the Son, and the Holy Spirit as Jesus in his Great Commission in Matthew 28:19–20 suggests.[4]

But how does one understand Trinity? Do we see the Trinity relationally as St Augustine suggested? Augustine's concept of *persona est relatio* is still widely used in Christian traditions despite major problems.[5] I suggest seeing the three persons of the Trinity as subjects.[6] A subject is defined out of its nature as well as in its relation to others. Jürgen Moltmann proves in his writings that such a concept overcomes the potential reductions of the Augustinian concept.[7] Each person of the Trinity is seen in this model in his own nature as well as in relation to the two others.

It was the church father, John Damaskin (675–749),[8] who first suggested the concept.[9] He described the Trinity as an eternal cycle, a *perichoresis*, in Greek "a round dance." According to Damaskin each person of the Trinity is vitally existing in the other two without losing his own identity. Miroslav Volf calls such a construct "reciprocal interiority."[10] We find this type of thinking predominantly in the Johannine writings. John sees the Father in the Son and the Son in the Father (John 17:21). Divine unity is an act of interiority.

Nobody has ever expressed this truth better than the Russian Orthodox painter Andrei Rublev (1360/1370–1430). His icon of the Holy Trinity, painted in 1425 for the famous monastery of the Holy Trinity in Radonezh near Moscow, is in all regards a highpoint of theological reflection on the issue.[11] The icon shows the divine persons around a table with a cup of offering indicating a discussion on the matter. All three are painted equal, there is no hierarchy,

---

3. Friedrich Hahn, *Theologie des Neuen Testaments*, Vol. 2 (Tübingen: Mohr-Siebeck, 2002), 290.

4. See more about the meaning of the baptism formula in regard to the Trinity in mission in Miroslav Volf, *After Our Likeness: The Church as the Image of the Trinity* (Grand Rapids: Eerdmans, 1998), 195.

5. See the discussion in Volf, *After His Likeness*, 204; Reimer, *Die Welt umarmen*, 152–153.

6. Volf, *After His Likeness*, 205.

7. Jürgen Moltmann, "Einführung: Einige Fragen der Trinitätslehre heute," in *In der Geschichte des dreieinigen Gottes: Beiträge zur trinitarischen Theologie* (München: Kaiser,1991), 11–21; Jürgen Moltmann, "Die einladende Einheit des dreieinigen Gottes," in *In der Geschichte des dreieinigen Gottes: Beiträge zur trinitarischen Theologie* (München: Kaiser, 1991),117–128.

8. For John of Damaskus, see BBKL, http://www.bautz.de/bbkl/j/Johannes_v_dam.shtml.

9. George Gladis, *Leading the Team-Based Church* (San Francisco: Jossey-Bass, 1999), 4ff.

10. Volf, *After His Likeness*, 209.

11. The icon is preserved in the Tretiakov Museum in Moscow.

no superiority, and the three are bound by a movement around the table of the Lord, the Eucharist.

Andrei Rublev's spirituality was formed in Radonezh.[12] The monastery was founded by St Sergius of Radonezh (1313/14 or 1321/22–1392),[13] and soon developed to be the centre of Russian Orthodox spirituality.[14] St Sergius in his spiritual journey followed the example of the hesychast Gregori Palamas (1296–1359), a monk from Mount Athos in Greece and the Archbishop of Thessaloniki, searching for contemplation and life in peace and obedience to God.[15] In the concept of the Trinity, Sergius found what he was searching for. His vita was written by his own disciple, the Moscovite Ephiphanius the Wise, between 1417–18, soon after the death of Sergius.[16] Sergius's theology was deeply Trinitarian. Epiphanius even says that the monastery of the Holy Trinity was constructed for the sake of "contemplating the Holy Trinity to overcome the hated fear which originated in the lustiness of the world."[17]

It is surprising how missional the Trinitarian theology of Sergius is. He declares that all theology must aim for salvation of the individual, which finds its fulfilment in the recovery of the original image of God, the lost *imago Dei* in the individual.[18] Sergius is fascinated by a possible *theosis* of all humanity.[19] Therefore the salvation of the individual results in his teachings, in love and service of the neighbour – the people and the nation – even if this means the sacrifice of one's own life.[20] In other words complete dedication, *kenosis,* precedes *theosis,* the ultimate transformation into the image of God. For Sergius the mission of God in the world is a kenotic action.[21] It aims towards spiritual

---

12. See for the spiritual socialization of Rublev N. A. Demina, *Andrei Rublev i chudozhniki yego kruga* (Moskva: Nauka, 1972); V. A. Polunin, *Mirovozreniye Andreya Rubleva* (Moskva: Moscow University Press, 1974); M. A. Ilyin, *Isskustvo moskovskoi Rusi Feofana Greka und Andreya Rubleva* (Moskva: Isskustvo, 1976); Vladimir Losski, *In the Image and Likeness of God* (New York, NY: SVS Press, 1997); etc.

13. See the discussion on the life dates of St Sergius in Johannes Reimer, "Mission des frühen russischen Mönchtums," Unpublished DTh thesis (Pretoria, SA: Unisa, 1994),161f.

14. Reimer, *Mission des frühen russichen Mönchtums*, 161.

15. See more on theology and work of Gregory in John Meyendorff, *A Study of Gregory Palamas* (London: Faith Press, 1964).

16. See for instance, Reimer, *Mission de frühen russichen Mönchtums*, 162.

17. Reimer, 164.

18. Reimer, 172.

19. Reimer, 174. Theofication does not mean deification of humanity, rather a restoration of the origional image of God in humanity.

20. Reimer, 176ff.

21. Reimer, 205.

enlightening of the nation.[22] In the theology of Sergius the centre of God's mission to the world is found in the Eucharist. Here is the place where all kenotic action finds its meaning. And this is what the icon of Rublev captures. He orders his figures cyclically following the symbolic language of Dionysius Areopagites who saw in the cyclical order an expression of eternity.[23] The three are in an eternal unity concerned with the salvation of the world that they made.[24]

Andrei Rublev: The Icon of the Holy Trinity of Heiligen Dreifaltigkeit

---

22. Reimer, 206ff.

23. See more about Dionisius in Wolfgang Müller, *Dionysios Areopagites und sein Wirken bis heute* (Dornach: Pforte Verlag, 1990).

24. See more in my interpretation of the icon in Johannes Reimer, "The Spirituality of Andrei Rublev's Icon of the Holy Trinity," in *Acta Theologica,* Supplementum 11 (2008): 166–180.

The triune God is a missionary God. How do the authors of the New Testament capture this very thought? Let's examine some of the New Testament passages in this regard.

4.2. *Missio Patri* – Laying Foundations

God is engaged with the world. Why? What motivates his missionary heart? The simplest answer given in the New Testament is – God loves the world he made, and his love to the world forces his divine engagement. Love to the world is the strongest motive behind the *missio Dei*.[25] Love is God's nature; he is love (1 John 4:8). To leave the world corrupted by Satan and to his destructive power would run totally against the very nature of God. The evangelist John quotes Jesus saying: "For God so loved the world that he gave his one and only Son, that whoever believes in him shall not perish but have eternal life" (John 3:16).

God the creator of the world loves his creation so much that he offers himself to save the world from destruction. Love as the basic motivation for God's saving action is already mentioned in the Old Testament. In Isaiah 63:7–9 we read:

> I will tell of the kindnesses of the LORD, the deeds for which he is to be praised, according to all the LORD has done for us – yes, the many good things he has done for Israel, according to his compassion and many kindnesses. He said, "Surely they are my people, sons who will not be false to me;" and so he became their Saviour. In all their distress he too was distressed, and the angel of his presence saved them. In his love and mercy he redeemed them; he lifted them up and carried them all the days of old.

God saves because he loves and has mercy. This is the main reason for his acts in the world, and his love is based on a decision he made long before the world was created. The apostle Paul states in Ephesians 1:3–6:

> Praise be to the God and Father of our Lord Jesus Christ, who has blessed us in the heavenly realms with every spiritual blessing in Christ. For he chose us in him before the creation of the world to be holy and blameless in his sight. In love he predestined us for adoption to sonship through Jesus Christ, in accordance with his

---

25. The theological discussion on mission motives is well presented in Walter Freitag, "Vom Sinn der Weltmission," *EMZ* 1 (1950): 1ff.

pleasure and will – to the praise of his glorious grace, which he
has freely given us in the One he loves.

God is a loving father and loved the world long before he made it. The
mission of God is anchored in his love for the world. Whoever joins God's
mission will enter a living stream of love flowing into the world. Loving God
always results in love for the neighbour. The two are interrelated (Mark 12:28–
34).[26] Change in the world presupposes love for the world. Only those who love
are ready to offer their own lives for the loved ones. God loves the world, and
this is the reason why he offers himself in the Son for the salvation of the world.

Love is the foundational ground of mission. David J. Bosch observes that
the first Christians were moved by love and John 3:16 can be seen as the main
foundational text of their mission.[27] Loving the neighbour was for Jesus and his
disciples the daily praxis of life. The German theologian Ulricht Wilkens, who
studied Jesus's preaching in the gospels in great detail, states: "All his sayings
seem to interpret the law of charity in Lev 19:18 with a view of its fulfilment
in life in the light of the kingdom of God."[28]

God loves the world and he comes back to it to establish his loving and just
reign. He created the world, and he knows best what is good for it and what
an autonomous world misses by going its own way. *Missio Dei* is concerned
with establishing God's kingdom in the world. Consequently, Jesus begins his
public activity with the words: "Repent, for the kingdom of heaven has come
near" (Matt 4:17). The reign of God and his kingdom are in fact "the central
themes of Jesus."[29] He preached the kingdom and proclaimed the presence of
the kingdom in his own person.[30] He healed the sick, liberated demoniacs,
and indicated signs of the approaching kingdom. No other text describes his
ministry better than Luke 4:16–19 when Jesus is in a synagogue in Nazareth and
reads Isaiah 61:1–2, a text which Jewish tradition has always interpreted in the

---

26. For the interpretation of the double commandment of love in the light of the kingdom
theology see Ulrich Wilckens, *Theologie des Neuen Testaments*, Vol. 1 (Neukirchen-Vluyn:
Neukirchener Verlag, 2002), 252ff.

27. David J. Bosch, *Transforming Mission: Paradigm Shifts in Theology of Mission*
(Maryknoll, NY: Orbis 1991), 208f.

28. Wilckens, *Theologie des Neuen Testaments*, 258.

29. Wilckens, 131.

30. Hans-Georg Kümmel, *Die Theologie des Neuen Testaments nach seinen Hauptzeugen
Jesus, Paulus, Johannes* (Göttingen: Vandenhoeck & Ruprecht, 1976), 30–35; Leonhard Goppelt,
Theologie des Neuen Testaments (Göttingen: Vandenhoeck & Ruprecht, 1978), 104ff.; Ulrich
Wilkens, *Theologie des Neuen Testament,* Vol. 1/3 (Neukirchen-Vluyn: Neukirchener Verlag,
2005), 131ff.

light of the coming Messiah that would introduce God's kingdom among his people. Jesus reads the text and "then he rolled up the scroll, gave it back to the attendant and sat down. The eyes of everyone in the synagogue were fastened on him. He began by saying to them, 'Today this Scripture is fulfilled in your hearing'" (Luke 4:20–21). In him, Jesus, this prophecy has been fulfilled. The year of Jubilee has come, God's kingdom is in the process of becoming reality, and this kingdom will cover all human existence. The political dimension of what is to follow is at hand. God's reign is real, his kingdom encompasses all spheres of life. Nothing is excluded. His kingdom is never only spiritual, but it is also material, social, and cultural. Jesus includes all those aspects of life when he introduces the kingdom in his famous parables.[31] God's all-encompassing reign on earth is what the disciples of Jesus are asked to pray for when Jesus teaches them: "This, then, is how you should pray: 'Our Father in heaven, hallowed be your name, your kingdom come, your will be done, on earth as it is in heaven'" (Matt 6:9–10).

God aims to transform the world so it becomes what he wants it to be. And the question is – what would a world ruled by God look like? Jesus did not talk much about the actual state in which the world under the reign of God is to be imagined. The only qualification he gives is – the world in the kingdom of God will be *new*.[32] He refers to the prophets, who also imagined the eschatological world as a new world. For instance, Isaiah hears God saying, "See, I am doing a new thing! Now it springs up; do you not perceive it? I am making a way in the wilderness and streams in the wasteland" (Isa 43:19). Jesus refers to Isaiah again and again; his theology of God's kingdom reflects his prophecy. Compare, for instance, the teaching of Jesus about the eschatological feast in Matthew 8:11, Mark 14:25, and Luke 22:29 with the feast God has prepared for the nations at the end of times as Isaiah sees it (Isa 25:6). Jesus obviously refers to the teachings of the prophet on the kingdom,[33] and his listeners understood him well. In their imagination they have seen a world reconciled with God as described in Isaiah 65:17–25. Here God promises:

> See, I will create new heavens and a new earth. The former things
> will not be remembered, nor will they come to mind. But be glad

---

31. Wilckens, *Theologie des Neuen Testaments*, 163–183; see also Robert Farrar, *Kingdom, Grace, Judgement: Paradox, Outrage, and Vindication in the Parables of Jesus* (Grand Rapids: Eerdmans, 1985), and others.

32. See for instance Mark 2:24.

33. More about the correlation between the teachings of Jesus and the prophet Isaiah in Wilkens, *Theologie*, 134ff.

and rejoice forever in what I will create, for I will create Jerusalem to be a delight and its people a joy. I will rejoice over Jerusalem and take delight in my people; the sound of weeping and of crying will be heard in it no more.

Never again will there be in it an infant who lives but a few days, or an old man who does not live out his years; the one who dies at a hundred will be thought a mere child; the one who fails to reach a hundred will be considered accursed. They will build houses and dwell in them; they will plant vineyards and eat their fruit. No longer will they build houses and others live in them, or plant and others eat. For as the days of a tree, so will be the days of my people; my chosen ones will long enjoy the work of their hands. They will not labour in vain, nor will they bear children doomed to misfortune; for they will be a people blessed by the LORD, they and their descendants with them. Before they call I will answer; while they are still speaking I will hear. The wolf and the lamb will feed together, and the lion will eat straw like the ox, and dust will be the serpent's food. They will neither harm nor destroy on all my holy mountain says the LORD.

God's new world as the prophet hears it is a socially just world. Whoever lives in this world will no longer live under oppression, will earn his living freely, will have a house for his family, and health for his body. It is a world in which blessing rules the day – God's blessing. It is a world in which God is present and where even the animals will experience harmony and peace. This world is God's missionary goal – a world under his rule – his kingdom. And the church is his chosen people – a people, a nation of the kingdom. The church is not God's kingdom, but belongs to the kingdom, as Ladd rightly claims.[34] Consequently the disciples of Jesus preached the gospel of the kingdom and not of the church (Acts 1:8; 8:12; 20:25; 28:23, 31). It was the kingdom they preached in the world (Matt 24:14).

In summary: God, the creator of the world, loves his creation and seeks for righteous ways to bring the world back under his divine and loving rule. It is the kingdom of God, which marks his missionary commission, the kingdom he seeks to establish on earth as it is in heaven.

---

34. George E. Ladd, *A Theology of the New Testament* (Grand Rapids: Eerdmans, 1974), 111. Compare also Wayne Grudem, *Systematic Theology: An Introduction to Biblical Doctrine* (Grand Rapids: Zondervan, 2004), 976.

4.3. *Missio Christi* – God's Way of Transformation

Jesus was God's best missionary.[35] Never ever has a human being been as close to God's heart as Jesus or as obedient to God's call. He totally identified with the will of God for his life, and therefore God gave him a name above all names (Phil 2:11). In fact, his name is the only name under the sun by which humans will be saved (Acts 4:12). He is the only appropriate way to God (John 14:6). Wherever the mission of God is attempted, Jesus will be the model to consider. To his own disciples the resurrected Christ said, "As the father has sent me, I am sending you" (John 20:21). The church is sent, as Jesus was sent. There is no extra sending for the church, no extra model of mission. He is both its message and its mission model. It is his body in the world (Eph 1:23). Nothing will be more important for the church on Earth than the *imitatio Christi,* the obedient following in the footsteps of Jesus.

So what was the mission of Jesus? How did he accomplish the task? Let's consider the following

a. The mission of Jesus began with incarnation. In John 1:1–6, 9–14 we read:

> In the beginning was the Word, and the Word was with God, and the Word was God. He was with God in the beginning. Through him all things were made; without him nothing was made that has been made. In him was life, and that life was the light of all mankind. The light shines in the darkness, and the darkness has not overcome it . . .
>
> The true light that gives light to everyone was coming into the world. He was in the world, and though the world was made through him, the world did not recognize him. He came to that which was his own, but his own did not receive him. Yet to all who did receive him, to those who believed in his name, he gave the right to become children of God – children born not of natural descent, nor of human decision or a husband's will, but born of God.
>
> The Word became flesh and made his dwelling among us. We have seen his glory, the glory of the one and only Son, who came from the Father, full of grace and truth.

---

35. Samuel Escobar, *La Palabra: Vida de la Iglesia* (El Paso: Baptist Spanish Publishing House, 2006), 97.

In Jesus, God himself becomes flesh in order to reveal to us the glory of God. Incarnation marks the point of total dedication, the *kenosis* (Greek), the emptying of himself as Jesus (Phil 2:7). Here the authors of the New Testament see the "focal point of *missio Dei*."[36] God's word for salvation, his final and ultimate concept to save the world, is Jesus (Heb 1:1–2). Jesus is first of all a man like us, a Jew from the Jews, in everything tempted like us, but without sin (Heb 4:15). Born in Bethlehem, he grew up in Nazareth with his parents Mary and Joseph;[37] he is, in every regard, a member of the social and cultural community of his nation.

b. Incarnation is an act of dedication to service the people of Israel. He is the Ebed Yahweh, the promised suffering servant who would come and save his nation by serving them, carrying their sin and their sickness (Isa 53:4–6). The gospels are full of stories showing the reader how human his life and ministry was. Just consider his first miracle in Cana. At a wedding celebration, he turns water into wine because the celebrating family runs out of wine (John 2:1–11). Jesus brings joy into the feast. He heals the sick, frees spirit-possessed people from demonic oppression, feeds the hungry, and cares for the wounded. His words are followed by deeds (Luke 9:11; Acts 10:36–38). He speaks about the kingdom and demonstrates the power of God's kingdom in what he does. "The healthy are not in need of a doctor, the sick are," Jesus says and he adds: "The son of man has not come in order to be served, but to serve" (Matt 20:28). He is God's servant (Luke 22:27). God meets us humans in the Man, Jesus of Nazareth. Whoever will in future search for God will find him in the Son of man, Jesus (John 1:18; 14:9). Mission, as Jesus sees it, is a matter of servanthood. He serves and he teaches his disciples to do the same (John 13:13–17).

c. Jesus serves to transform. In Jesus, God reconciles the world to himself (2 Cor 5:18–19). Salvation is what he brings to the world (Acts 4:12). With him God's promise of Jubilee becomes reality (Isa 61:1–2; Luke 4:18). The American theologian, John Howard Yoder (1927–1997), strongly believed that the year Jesus was referring to as Jubilee would have actually been one of the fiftith years in the history of Israel.[38] As far as we know Israel never kept the law of God in this regard. In the centuries Jubilee became a synonym for the

---

36. Stuart Murray, *Church Planting: Laying Foundation* (Carlisle, Cumbria: Paternoster, 2001), 42.

37. This does not mean that Joseph was his natural father. As we know Joseph adopted Jesus as his son.

38. Murray, 67.

messianic eschatological kingdom. Now Jesus was connecting his ministry to the Jubilee, claiming to be the promised Messiah. In his excellent book, *The Politics of Jesus*,[39] Yoder points to how the social and political dimensions of Jesus's ministry closely related to the Jubilee narrative. According to Yoder, Jesus introduces with his ministry a movement of social change.[40] He even claims the teachings of Jesus are normative for Christian social ethics[41] and must be understood against the Jubilee law in the Old Testament.[42]

  d. Transformation introduced by Jesus points towards the kingdom of God. Jesus proclaims the gospel of the kingdom of God. His ministry as we have seen above is kingdom centred.

  e. Jesus creates a new people of the kingdom – the church. To Peter, who realizes that Jesus is the Messiah of God, Jesus says, "You are Simon Peter and on this rock I will build my church and the fortress of hell will not prevail against her" (Matt 16:18). His people are a new holy nation, a royal priesthood (1 Pet 2:9–10).

  In summary: *Missio Christi* is God's method and model to establish his kingdom. It includes incarnational service and proclamation with the aim to transform all life under the reign of God.

4.4. *Missio Spiritus* – God's Praxis of Transformation

The mission of the church started on Pentecost. With the coming of the Holy Spirit in Jerusalem[43] both the church and its mission were born. It is the Spirit of God who heads up mission and builds the church in the world. Scripture leaves no question in this regard.[44] The church is founded and sustained by the Holy Spirit.[45] The Spirit is the implementer of the mission of God. It is through the Spirit that men believe in Jesus (1 Cor 12:3), through the Spirit they are formed into one body of Christ, the Church (1 Cor 12:13), through the Spirit they receive gifts and ministries (1 Cor 12:4–5). The church is called a fellowship of the Spirit, a house of God (1 Cor 3:16), a "spiritual house" (1 Pet 2:5), the place where God lives (1 Cor 6:19).

---

39. John Howard Yoder, "*Die Politik Jesu*," (Maxdorf: *Agape Verlag*, 1981).
40. Yoder, *Die Politik Jesu*, 25–26.
41. Yoder, 21.
42. Yoder, 59–69.
43. Acts 2:1–36.
44. David Ewert, *Holy Spirit in the New Testament* (Scottdale: Herald Press, 1983), 200f.
45. Ewert, *Holy Spirit*, 201.

The mission of God in the world is directly related to what the Spirit does. In fact, he is the Lord of mission (2 Cor 3:17). What does this mean in practical terms?

a. The Holy Spirit is the **creator fidae,** *the founder of faith.* When Jesus promised his disciples that he would send them the Spirit, he stressed the fact that it would be he who would come to convince the world of sin, righteousness, and justice (John 16:8); he who would lead the disciples in all truth reminding them of all he, Jesus, had taught them (John 14:26; 16:13). He commanded them not to leave Jerusalem until the Holy Spirit fell on them and made them witnesses unto the ends of the world (Acts 1:8). For Jesus it is clear – a relationship to him is only possible through the Spirit. The apostle Paul underlines this in 1 Corinthians 12:3 by claiming that no one will be able to call Jesus Lord except through the Holy Spirit. The Spirit of God is the "point of departure of faith."[46] Whoever longs for the fellowship with God will have to be born again (John 3:5), an experience of being baptized in the Holy Spirit (Titus 3:5). Only those people who are sealed with the Spirit (Eph 1:13), who possess the Spirit (Rom 8:9) are able to live in the power and glory of God the Father and do what Jesus has commanded them to do (John 16:7). It is as Clowney rightly says "the Spirit who leads to Christ."[47] Without the Holy Spirit there can be no relationship to Jesus the Christ. And without it there will be no relationship to God the Father. Only those who are led by the Spirit of God are children of God. He gives clarity to our spirit that we are children of God (Rom 8:14–16).

b. The Holy Spirit is the **creator ecclesiae,** *the founder of the church.* As we have seen, the church was born on the day of Pentecost. Already the prophets of the Old Testament had related the renewal of God's people to the coming of the Holy Spirit. (See for instance: Isa 32:15; 44:3; Ezek 11:19; 36:26–32; 37:14; Joel 3:1–2.) Peter consequently declares to the Jews – gathered from all the nations in Jerusalem at the day of Pentecost, that the outpouring of the Spirit is a fulfilment of prophecy. And he urges them to repent (Acts 2:37–40). And five thousand do repent and are baptized in the name of Jesus. They are the first to join the church of Christ. The church is born in the presence of the Holy Spirit.[48] And it is born from all the nations gathered in Jerusalem. The nation of God becomes a universal reality. The disciples of Jesus coming from

---

46. Gordon Fee, *Der Geist Gottes und die Gemeinde* (Erzhausen: Leuchter Verlag, 2005), 129.

47. Edmund P. Clowney, *The Church* (Leicester: IVP, 1995), 51.

48. Gerhard Lohfink, *Wie hat Jesus Gemeinde gewollt?* (Freiburg-Basel-Wien: Herder, 1982), 96.

the Jewish nation are now being called to go to all nations of the world (Acts 1:8). Through Pentecost the disciples of Jesus receive their global messianic identity.[49] He, the Holy Spirit, is the creator of the new collective, the new social institute called the body of Christ, building the actual structure of God's people on earth (1 Cor 12:13). This body is continuing what Jesus started in the world to the praise of his glory (Eph 1:3–10). This body is spiritual, does not belong to the world around us, but it is in the world and, as such, *for* the world (John 17:17–18). The church is spiritual, but it is also a social structure. It is not separate from the world, but it is still in the world and only here does it have its divine calling. The Spirit of God builds the church as a universal reality. Everybody in the world is welcomed; no one is excluded. He provides his gifts to every person coming to faith in Christ (1 Cor 12:4–6), opening in this way a place of service and dignity in the kingdom.

c. The Holy Spirit as dominus missii, *the Lord of mission.* "Where the Spirit of God is involved, there is witness in the world and powerful proclamation of the gospel."[50] Jesus indicates this to his disciples pointing to the fact that the experience of the Spirit will lead to witnessing in Jerusalem, Judea . . . and to the ends of the world (Acts 1:8). The church begins as a witnessing community sent to all the nations of the world. Jesus himself grants his disciples his Spirit before he sends them to the mission the Father has sent him (John 20:21). Wherever his disciples will join his mission they will do so in the Spirit and power (1 Cor 2:4). Christians are servants of the new covenant, "not the covenant of the letter but of the Spirit" (2 Cor 3:6). And he, the Holy Spirit, is the Lord of God's mission, implementing what the Father wants in the way Jesus has suggested (2 Cor 3:17).

In summary: The mission of the Spirit of God is to create faith in people and join them into a missionary people for realization of God's kingdom in the world.

4.5. The Mission of the Triune God

God is a missionary God, and he revealed himself to us as Father, Son, and Holy Spirit. His self-revelation is interrelated. As his nature is basically a reciprocal interiority, his mission is equally interconnected. What the Father wants, the Son puts into a system, and the Spirit into praxis. The cycle of

49. Jürgen Roloff, "*Die Kirche des Neuen Testaments*," NTD, Ergänzungsreihe 10 (Göttingen: Nandehoeck & Ruprecht, 1993), 63–64.

50. Hahn, *Theologie des Neuen Testaments*, 280.

missio Dei consists of God who lays the foundation, Jesus who determines the methodology, and the Holy Spirit who leads the praxis.

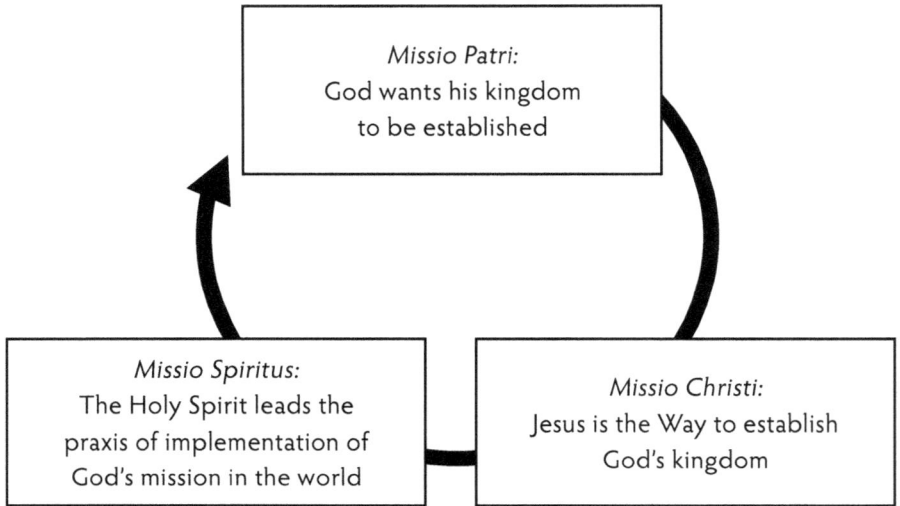

The Divine Perichoresis of Mission

4.6. Is God's Mission Political?

We come back to the original question of this inquiry: Is the mission of God political? He made the world to serve his purpose. He is concerned with corruption and sin in the world since humans disobeyed him and allowed Satan to influence them. God is concerned with his rule over the world. He wants his kingdom back, a kingdom in which justice and righteousness rule. Is this political? Is the realization of God's reign in the world political? God wants to turn the world around us up-side-down, transform every bit of it. Is this politics?

Jesus came to announce that the kingdom of God is near, proclaiming God's reign – realized in his own person and available to every person in the world willing to follow him in every aspect of life. Is this political? Is his alternative community of God's chosen people – those who refuse to follow the established pattern of the world, but instead, orient themselves on a model of living suggested by Jesus – political?

Is the praxis of the Holy Spirit – the one who is the Lord of the *missio Dei* in the world and who is sent to convince the world of its wrong ways in culture and society and turn it back to God and his rigorousness and justice – political? It is surely spiritual. Can spirituality be political?

The answer is yes, it is. How else would we name all the transformative and life-changing action of God in the world? As soon as people suggest cultural and societal change, we name their action political. Is not the transformative mission of God so much more political? It is, and it has immediate consequences for the mission of the church in the world. We shall explore those in detail by looking at the nature and the mission of the church.

5

The Nature and Mission
of the Church of Christ

5.1. Called to Be Responsible

What is church? A simple question and easily answered by Christians. Martin Luther even claimed that every child of seven years old knows the answer.[1] In reality, however, the question is much more complicated, as the amount of literature on the nature of the church proves. We are well advised to go back to the New Testament for an adequate answer.

The church of Christ is first and foremost *his* church. So what did Jesus say his church is to be? In Matthew 16:17–18 we read, "Jesus replied, 'Blessed are you, Simon son of Jonah, for this was not revealed to you by flesh and blood, but by my Father in heaven. And I tell you that you are Peter, and on this rock I will build my church, and the gates of Hades will not overcome it.'" Jesus says he is going to build his church. Whoever defines church will have to conform to what Jesus says a church is. In other words a church is only a church of Christ when it conforms to the community designed by Jesus. Jesus defined his church as *ecclesia*, the Greek term used in our passage. It contains two words: *ec* for out and *caleo* for calling and stands for *the called out*. In the ancient world, the Greeks used the term for a political gathering of all citizens of a given city with the right of voice.[2] The magistrate called all of them out for a parliamentarian meeting to discuss and to vote on crucial issues in the life of

---

1. Martin Luther, "Schmalkaldische Artikel," in *WA BSKL* 50: 250.

2. L. Coenen, "Kirche," in *Theologisches Begriffslexikon zum Neuen Testament*, eds. L. Coenen, E. Beireuther, H. Biedenhand, 3rd ed. (Wuppertal: Brockhaus, 1972), 784.

the city. *Ecclesia* means therefore, literally translated, a politically responsible assembly called out to vote on issues of life in the community.

It is rather unexpected to use the term for a religious gathering. The Jews named their religious meetings *synagogue*, a similar term to *ecclesia* with more or less an exclusive religious meaning. This is also the term used in the Septuagint (LXX), the Greek translation of the Old Testament, for religious meetings of God's people. *Ecclesia*, in contrast, is translated by the Hebrew expression *kahal Jahwe*, generally used to describe the gathering of Israel for political reasons, for instance when the kings of Israel assembled the tribes in order to enter war.[3] Until today *kahal* is used in Israel for an assembly gathered to decide socio-economic questions.

The question at hand is – did Jesus use the term accidentally, or rather consciously?[4] And if so, what does the fact that the term was used mean for the theology and mission of a church? I believe that the New Testament is God's inspired word, and I can't see any ill use of terminology. Jesus meant what is said.

Examine, for instance, the idea of God's new people in the gospel of Matthew. Jesus calls his disciples "salt of the earth and light of the world" (Matt 5:13–15), expecting the light to be placed at the highest spot in the city in order that it might shine for everybody. He sends his disciples to all the *ethne* of the world, commissioning them to disciple the *ethne* and teach them to live in accordance to his teachings (Matt 28:19–20). *Ethnos* is usually translated as nation. The original meaning, however, is *people as a socio-cultural space.*[5] The Great Commission targets nations not individuals, social and cultural space not individual lives. They might be included, but the commission goes far beyond individuals to the community, to the nations with all their culture.

In the light of these texts, *ecclesia* is called out of the world to become light for the world, accepting responsibility for the world and transforming the world into a place according to the teaching of Jesus on the kingdom of God. It is a consequence that in such a transformed space hell will never prevail in the gates of the city, as Matthew 16:18 states. The gates stand for the place where decisions in the city were made. It was the place where the local *ecclesia* met.

3. H. P. Müller, "qahal Versammlug," in *THAT*, ed. Ernst Jenni. Vol. 2 (München: Kaiser Verlag, 1979), 609–619.

4. See more in my discussion of the term in Johannes Reimer, *Die Welt umarmen, Theologie des gesellschaftsrelevanten Gemeindebaus,* Transformationsstudien, Vol. 1 (Marburg: Francke Verlag, 2009), 36–41.

5. See more in Gerhard Kittel, Gerhard Friedrich, and Geoffrey W. Bromiley, *Theological Dictionary of the New Testament*, abridged in 1 vol. (Grand Rapids: Eerdmans, 1985), 201–202.

Jesus's promise is powerful: he builds a church, and hell will not rule in the gates of the city.

The *ecclesia* is, in all regards, a religious body with a clear call to accept responsibility for the well-being of a given community. It is important to see that the term is used in the New Testament exclusively for a local community.[6] The church is locally defined whenever the term is used in singular. It is the church in Jerusalem, Rome, or Antioch. Referring to a region, the province of Asia for instance, the term will always appear in plural. *Ecclesia* is a local institution. Its light must shine locally as brightly as possible to give everybody in the place orientation.

Last, *ecclesia* as light of the city does not simply take part in the conversation of what builds up community. It is the light of the city because people see its good deeds and glorify the Lord (Matt 5:16). The *ecclesia* proclaims in words and deeds; it is a serving community. It does not simply orient the community towards a better place of living. The church works actively to build community through its good deeds. By doing so, it becomes an agent of evangelism. Neighbours in the community will see the good works and react by praising our Father in heaven, says Jesus. This presupposes, however, that the neighbours know the church by name, know why it does what it does, and attribute the good deeds to its faith and lastly to God the Father. The community involvement of the church must be clearly marked by its spiritual and religious identity. This makes the church more than an agent of social change. It will be seen as a prophetic voice of God and a priestly assistance of a god-related people, a royal priesthood, a new nation (1 Pet 2:9–10), an institution of justice and righteousness (2 Cor 5:21).

In summary: the church, as Jesus saw it, is a public institution. It is an assembly gathered out of the world for transformative action for the world. It is clearly not of the world, as Jesus says (John 17:16), and it does not conform to the pattern of the world (Rom 12:2), but is in the world and for the world

Is this political? Is community transformation a political act? And if so – what kind of political act?

5.2. Sent to Be Light of the World

Jesus builds his church for a purpose. The apostle Paul summarizes the calling of Christians in remarkable words. In Ephesians 2:10 we read, "For we are God's

---

6. Reimer, *Die Welt umarmen*, 38–39.

handiwork, created in Christ Jesus to do good works, which God prepared in advance for us to do." No, the church of Christ does not exist accidentally. It has a mission, and its mission must follow the mission of the Master. In John 20:21, the resurrected Christ says to his disciples, "As the father has sent me – I am sending you." The missionary mandate of the church of Christ must follow his own calling.

And how was Jesus sent? In the previous chapter we discussed his calling. He is sent to proclaim God's kingdom in accordance with the Jubilee Year of the Lord (Luke 4:18–19). John Stott reflects on the ministry of Jesus and states: "The Kingdom of God he proclaimed and inaugurated was a radical new and different social organisation, whose values and standards challenge those of the old and fallen community. . . . It offered an alternative to the status quo. His Kingship, moreover, was perceived as a challenge to Caesar and he was, therefore accused of sedition."[7] Whatever Jesus did, the public read political action into his life and ministry. It is understandable when Dr Joseph D'Souza calls Jesus a "dissident."[8]

Sent as Jesus was sent, the disciples of Christ followed the same message. Soon after Pentecost they were selling their property and caring for the poor and the needy in Jerusalem. Barnabas, for instance, was a Levite who owned land – contrary to how the law commissioned Levites to live. Becoming a follower of Jesus, he does what he would have to do in the year of Jubilee – sell all his land and bring the money to the feet of the apostles (Acts 4:36–37).

The acts of the disciples and their message had an incredible impact on the city of Jerusalem. Daily, people were becoming followers of Jesus, and consequently the elite reacted against them. In Acts 4:23–31 we read the beautiful prayer of the persecuted followers of Jesus in Jerusalem:

> On their release, Peter and John went back to their own people and reported all that the chief priests and the elders had said to them. When they heard this, they raised their voices together in prayer to God. "Sovereign Lord," they said, "you made the heavens and the earth and the sea, and everything in them. You spoke by the Holy Spirit through the mouth of your servant, our father David:

---

7. Stott, *New Issues*, 14.

8. Dr Joseph D'Souza and Benedict Rogers, *On the Side of the Angels: Justice, Human Rights and Kingdom Mission* (Colorado Springs: Authentic, 2007), 6.

"'Why do the nations rage
and the peoples plot in vain?
The kings of the earth rise up
and the rulers band together
against the Lord
and against his anointed one.'"

Indeed Herod and Pontius Pilate met together with the Gentiles and the people of Israel in this city to conspire against your holy servant Jesus, whom you anointed. They did what your power and will had decided beforehand should happen. Now, Lord, consider their threats and enable your servants to speak your word with great boldness. Stretch out your hand to heal and perform signs and wonders through the name of your holy servant Jesus."

After they prayed, the place where they were meeting was shaken. And they were all filled with the Holy Spirit and spoke the word of God boldly.

No, the disciples of Christ did not run away from Jerusalem when facing persecution. On the contrary – they served the needy and proclaimed the gospel of the kingdom as their Lord Jesus did, and their good deeds led masses to become followers of Jesus, praising the Father in heaven, exactly as Jesus commanded them to do, becoming the light of the world and the salt of the earth (Matt 5:13–16). Soon the Spirit of the Lord led them to cross the borders of Israel and expand their mission to the furthest corners of the Roman Empire in full accordance with the Great Commission of Jesus. It was him, who gathered them all to the mount in Galilee to commission them "to make disciples of all nations, baptizing them in the name of the Father and of the Son and of the Holy Spirit, and teaching them to obey everything I have commanded you" (Matt 28:19–20).

It is of great importance to see what this commission encompasses. Jesus commands his disciples to disciple *nations*. They are not just responsible for a few individuals. No, their task is to lead nations to accept the kingdom of God and live by the standards Jesus was teaching them. In praxis this means no less than to transform the socio-cultural space nations live in. And this is highly political.

Commissioned people will one day be held responsible for what they have accomplished. Asked what would happen when he returns back to earth, Jesus tells his disciples the parable of the three labourers hired by a landowner who gave each of them talents and then left the country advising them to go and multiply what they had received (Matt 25:1–46). Upon his return he holds them accountable and finds the one who has not done the job and sends him away. The other two are invited to take their inheritance and join the kingdom. Asked what caused the gracious invitation, Jesus replies, "For I was hungry and you gave me something to eat, I was thirsty and you gave me something to drink. I was a stranger and you invited me in. I needed clothes and you clothed me, I was sick and you looked after me, I was in prison and you came to visit me."

And the privileged surprized by his words asked him. "When did we see you hungry and feed you, or thirsty and give you something to drink? When did we see you a stranger and invited you in, or needing clothes and clothe you? When did we see you sick or in prison and go and visit you?" And the King will reply, "Whatever you did for one of the least of these brothers of mine, you did for me."

The essence of the parable is clear – God's people are in the world to care for those in need. Joseph D'Souza summarizes correctly: "Unless and until Christian life and witness actually becomes involved in individual lives and society, we cannot authentically carry out kingdom mission in this world."[9] It is your task to care for the least, the last and the lost, to promote the human dignity of our fellow men and women.[10]

In conclusion: The church of Christ being *ecclesia* is by its very nature called to accept responsibility for the world around it, transforming its community into disciples of Christ and teaching them to live according to the values of God's kingdom. This means its mission will always be political. Being missionary by its very nature and called to transform society, it cannot withdraw from the world. The church is not *of the world*, but as Jesus claimed, *in the world*, where its task is. Leaving the world equals leaving the commission of Christ and losing its nature as the church of Christ.

---

9. D'Souza, *On the Side*, 17.

10. D'Souza, 25.

6

The Political Task of the Church

6.1. Politically Responsible Institution

The church of Christ is a socio-political institution and its mission has a genuine political dimension, whether it likes it or not.[1] To negate this means to misunderstand the nature and the mission of the *ecclesia*. The German theologian Schwarz states: "A Christian Church may never ask whether she has to accept her political responsibility, she has rather to ask how to fulfil her political mandate."[2] To know how to fulfil a task, we have to determine what the political involvement of the church encompasses.

The history of the church proves to us that there is a long history of socio-political involvement of the church and of individual Christians.[3]

Is the church called to remove the rulers of the world from their throne and rule instead? The memories of what happened in the world when it attempted to do so are rather dark. In the New Testament there is no mention of the church becoming the new governing agent for the world. Instead the apostle Paul points to governing authorities established by God himself (Rom 13:1–2), and they are not identified with the church. What then does it mean for the church to become an agent of transformation in practical terms? Reading Scripture we might underline some crucial observations.

The *ecclesia* is a royal priesthood (1 Pet 2:9–10). It is God's voice in the world. It proclaims the gospel of the kingdom of God. It does not rule the

---

1. Grant Osborne, *Romans* (Downers Grove: IVP, 2004), 320.

2. Fritz Schwarz and Christian Schwarz, *Überschaubare Gemeinde* (Gladbeck: Aussaat, 1980), 136.

3. See for instance J. W. de Gruchy, *Christianity and Democracy* (David Philip: Cape Town, 1995).

world, but rather calls the world to submit under the rule of God. It prays his kingdom to become reality on earth as it is in heaven. Its greatest desire is the kingdom of God (Matt 6:33). As such it does not aim for power, but rather critically engages all powers of the world, pointing them to God who has the ultimate say in all matters of life. No, the church does not desire to rule, rather it seeks God's rule on earth. This specifies its political task in three dimensions as (a) God's priest in the world; (b) God's transformative agent of change; (c) God's prophetic voice in culture and society.

6.2. A Communal Priest

The church is a royal *priesthood* (1 Pet 2:9–10). It is never the king, but it serves the King of kings. It is God's chosen people, "chosen for blessing"[4] and "chosen for all."[5] As such it represents before God the people among whom it lives and, on the other hand, represents God whom it serves to the community in which it is. It is a living sign of the kingdom among the people.

First the church brings the society in which it is located to the living God. It knows that all life is only possible because of God's grace, so it prays for grace and blessing for the people and governing institutions in society, culture, and economy. Knowing that only blessed politics are life giving politics, it will invest time and strength in intercession. And knowing how weak and misleading humans are, it will plead with God for yet more grace and forgiveness for those in society who transgress and sin. It is the priestly prayer of the church that keeps the world from a complete collapse. Where strong churches pray for their societies, there communities change in every regard. But where churches do not pray for their neighbours and community, forces of darkness take over. The political mission of the church starts with intercession for all agents in the political space. It is God's chosen priest for the world around it.

But the priestly church will not only appear in front of God interceding for the community. Second, it is called to be God's ambassador of reconciliation acting in the name and authority of Christ, proclaiming to the world complete restoration of its relationship with the Creator through salvation in Christ (2 Cor 5:18–20). It lives among the people as an alternative, reconciled with God's community of people, a fellowship of brothers and sisters, a family of God in which righteousness and justice is present (2 Cor 5:21). Where it is, darkness

---

4. Wright, *The Mission of God*, 191.
5. Wright, 222.

moves away, because it is the light of the world (Matt 5:14–15). Here in its presence people may see and experience God.

As God's priest the church will ask God and answer the questions of the people and will speak out whatever judgment God makes over the structures of society and culture. It will never condone those who introduce selfishness and corruption to their people. It will name the unrighteousness and confront injustice. It will stay with the poor and weak even when this means offering itself for the sake of the oppressed. The world around it will know that there is a priest in their midst who will advocate for them without fear. It does so out of a deep sense of love for its neighbours and the knowledge of its calling to proclaim God's justice to all people. Loving God presupposes love to the neighbours. This is what the great commandment of Jesus is all about. To a Jewish teacher asking Jesus for the greatest commandments of all Jesus replied: "'Love the Lord your God with all your heart and with all your soul and with all your mind.' This is the first and greatest commandment. And the second is like it: 'Love your neighbour as yourself.' All the Law and the Prophets hang on these two commandments" (Matt 22:37– 40).

The church as a community priest is light and salt in the community and its mission is catalytic. It does not rule; it models and serves. But as salt will never lose its impact dissolving in water, so the church will impact community as long as it is the salt of the earth. And as light always wins against darkness, the church in a city will protect the community from forces of darkness. As long as the church is what God wants it to be, Jesus says: "You are the salt of the earth. But if the salt loses its saltiness, how can it be made salty again? It is no longer good for anything, except to be thrown out and trampled underfoot." The loss of its mission results in the loss of any societal validity. Where the church does not accept its political priestly role as a communal priest, it will soon become unattractive and irrelevant. This is a sad reality in many countries of the world.

To be a communal priest is a high calling, but it does not mean that the church must become a *societa perfecta*, a perfect society. It is a human reality, and as such, a learning community in which grace is not only preached but also experienced. You may find among its members, people in urgent need of forgiveness because of their sin. But in deference to the world, members of the church know God and turn to him for grace. Being transformed they become priestly agents of transformation for others. The priestly church is a transforming agent, changing lives by being changed through God its Lord.

6.3. A Royal Servant

The church of Christ is a priest among the people, a *royal* priest. It acts in the name and in the power and authority of the king. It is not king itself, however; it does what the king commands it to do. Being royal means all issues of government matter to it. It has responsibility to create a meaningful space of living and the authority to put its concepts into real practice. Being royal gives it the highest authority available. But it will not exorcize its power by force. Nowhere in Scripture is the church asked to govern society. God has placed governments in each nation for this. They are God's *servants* to rule nations (Rom 13:1).

The church is rather a royal *servant* to serve nations. It does not act out of the power of the office, it acts by love. It does not reach its transformative goals by force but rather by serving people in need. It does not fight its enemies, but rather serves them in love just as the wise Solomon taught (Prov 25:21–22), knowing that its real enemy is not people, not "flesh and blood" as the apostle Paul says, but the forces of darkness (Eph 6:12).

As God's agent of transformation, the church will care for the poor, feed the hungry, work for freedom of those in prison, support the oppressed, and find ways to set them free. Where it is, the blind will recover their sight, the lame will walk, and the kingdom of God will take shape in the midst of community. It will love all, serve all, and by doing so, glorify its Father in heaven. It does so because it loves its neighbour as itself. The Croatian theologian Peter Kuzmic rightfully summarizes: "There is no authentic mission without the motivation of love and compassion."[6] The model it operates from is redemption, and this is based in the exodus narrative of the Old Testament, leading to complete restoration pictured in the theology of Jubilee as it is expressed in the Old Testament.[7]

All of this by definition is political involvement. All of this is done among the people and for the people. And all of this is the work of a servant. Political involvement of the church is, therefore, *diaconic in nature*. It changes community by serving the community in love. Yes, the church will name the issues and take position where injustice dominates community, and no, the

---

6. Peter Kuzmic, "Justice, Mercy and Humility," in *Justice, Mercy and Humility: Intergral Mission and the Poor*, ed. Tim Chester (London: Paternoster Press, 2002), 158.

7. See the discussion in Wright, *The Mission of God*, 265–323; Roland Hardmeier, *Kirche ist Mission: Auf dem Weg zu einem ganzheitlichen Missionsverständnis* (Schwarzenfeld: Neufeld Verlag, 2009), 89–140.

church will not engage in combat. It prefers rather to die for an enemy than erase the life of others.

Whenever the church of Christ allowed political power structures to take over its engagement, whenever it desired the throne, it soon became worse than those it replaced. Just think of Roman Catholic Popes during the Middle Ages, or the Byzantine symphony between the church and state, the Moscovite bloody rule of Tzar Ivan the Terrible, with the Russian Orthodox on his side, or the rule of Jan van Leyden, the self-proclaimed king of the Anabaptist kingdom of Münster in Germany. The stories are all similar – the church determines the regime, exorcizes political power by force, and loses its legitimate right to be a royal priesthood that serves. It loses its crucial role of transforming the world around it to be a better place of living ruled by the values of God's kingdom.

6.4. A Prophetic Witness

The church of Christ is called to be a communal priest in royal service proclaiming the gospel of the kingdom. It has to raise its voice for the poor, the imprisoned, oppressed, and needy. It does not favour people, as God does not choose some and reject others (Rom 2:11). He wants all people on earth to be saved (1 Tim 2:4), so the church speaks for everybody. Its voice is the voice of a prophet, and it is the prophet to whom God entrusts his revelation, as Amos (3:7) states: "Surely the Lord God will do nothing, but he revealeth his secret unto his servants the prophets."

Prophets of the Old Testament were men and women through whom God revealed the past and present conditions the people were living in, naming the sin of father and son, mother and daughter, the king and his people. But at the same time prophets revealed God's salvific plan for the people for the future. Prophets were analytically geniuses, without any compromise and, at the same time, with a message of hope for the future. They spoke forth "the mind and counsel of God for repentance to be taught and righteousness to be preached in order to bring restoration, to heal (Matt 9:35)."[8]

Prophets acted in public. Amos, for instance, prophesized against societies that "trample the heads of the weak into the dust of the earth, and force the lowly out of the way" (Amos 2:7). His prophetic word was directed against unjust and oppressive rulers (Amos 3:9–10) and criminal judges (Amos 5:12; cf. Isa 1:23). Jeremiah boldly named the state of misery in society, blaming

---

8. http://www.angelfire.com/in/HisName/ (Last access: 23 August 2017).

the leading elite for it. He openly advocated for all the marginalized and the downtrodden, rebuking the leading class for their corrupt and evil practices (Jer 6:7–1; 8:8–13, 22). The prophet Isaiah focused on the evil practices of religious leaders (Isa 58:5–7). John the Baptist and then Jesus followed the prophets of the Old Testament in their public proclamation of truth (Luke 16:19–31). Jesus's prophetic ministry was clearly political.

The church of Christ is built on the foundation laid by apostles and prophets (Eph 2:20). This foundation is Jesus Christ (1 Cor 3:11) who comes into human lives in the spirit of prophecy (Rev 19:10). Consequently, the church is urged to make space for prophecy in its midst to promote edification of its members (Eph 4:29; 1 Thess 5:11, 19–21; 1 Cor 14:3–4, 31) and their witness in society (Eph 4:11–12). A "missionary church will stand on shoulders of prophets," states the Brazilian theologian Paolo Suess.[9] Where prophets act – life is promoted, transformation introduced, and human dignity restored.[10] The prophetic voice of the church shall not be suppressed (1 Thess 5:20). It reveals what is wrong, corrupt, sinful, and destructive, acting in bold humility. Nothing else is so much against the prophetic nature of the church as political correctness. Only when the church becomes unfaithful to the gospel, does it become an instrument of the status quo.[11] Prophets are fearless in naming the issues of the day, uncovering the life threats in society, confronting the rulers and structures with their wrongdoing and standing up against injustice. The prophetic church will always join the socio-political discourse on life issues of the day, not because it knows better, but because it is God's venue to speak his truth to people.

The prophetic church will speak up because the earth is of the Lord, and he is not only the creator but also the sustainer of the world. Any ecological, economic, cultural, and social development endangering life on earth is an issue he will speak to and with him his prophetic voice – the church. Any attempt of certain political forces to exploit habitats of humanity and creation will challenge God's action and cause the church to raise its voice against such forces. It is God's priest on earth, advocating for life for all creation. Egoistic and life-threatening exploitation of nature will raise its protest. Ideological decisions and politically oppressive systems will find the church voicing active

9. Paolo Suess, "Zur Prophetie im Horizont der Menschenwürde," in *Mission und Prophetie in Zeiten der Interkulturalität*, trans. by Mariano Delgado and Michael Sievernich, FS zum hundertjährigen Bestehen des Internationalen Instituts für missionswissenschaftliche Forschungen 1911–2011 (St Ottilien: EOS Verlag, 2011), 46.

10. Ibid., 39–40.

11. See René Padilla, *Mission between the Times: Essays on the Kingdom* (Grand Rapids: Eerdmans, 2010), 54

opposition. The church, as Jürgen Moltmann states, "intervenes critically and prophetically in the public affairs of a given society, and draws public attention, not to the church's own interest, but to God's kingdom, God's commandments and his righteousness."[12]

Biblical prophecy is a moral voice in the midst of a nation, but prophets were far more than critics only. Pronouncing judgment, they were also announcing ways of repentance and a new beginning. They were messengers of hope and a restored future under God's rule. They were calling the people to actively change their life, teaching them holy living under the lordship of God.

In the light of a prophetic ministry the Great Commission of Christ in Matthew 28:19–20 encourages active participation in transforming nations into a disciple of Christ. Teaching a nation all that was taught to the disciples, the church becomes an active agent of change and transformation of society, living a transformed life and teaching the public God's way of living and inviting them into a kingdom space ruled by the Spirit of God. It is crucial to see that the prophetic witness of the church requires the public appearance of kingdom living. The church must be placed at the highest point in a city in order that it may be light to all citizens. Prophetic living encourages interest in God's kingdom and intrigues society to listen to the prophetic voice. When people see the glory of God displayed in lives of Christians they may start desiring to experience the glory of God (John 1:1–14).

Prophetic witness is proclamation in life, deed, and word. Jesus is the best example of this. He used a variety of approaches to address the public: healing the sick, feeding the hungry, caring for the distressed, offering a different kind of fellowship, and, of course, preaching the gospel of the kingdom. The prophetic church will follow his example. It will also live prophetically as a living sign of the kingdom, invest itself in transformative action in community, and speak the gospel message to those who are still outside of God's grace.

6.5. The Place of Political Involvement

Ecclesia is a local institution. This is how the New Testament presents God's new people to us. Here in a local community it finds its main space of missionary action, and here its political involvement is a natural expression of what it is and wants. In the local city, placed in a prominent spot, seen from everywhere,

---

12. Jürgen Moltmann, *Experiences in Theology: Ways and Forms of Christian Theology*, trans. by M. Kohl (Fortress Press, Philadelphia, 2000).

it offers light to everyone, serving the people through its good deeds, and encouraging them to praise God (Matt 5:13–16).

There is no place under the sun where people have such easy and natural access to the church as in a community of neighbours. Here people see and observe the authenticity and holiness of God's sign of the kingdom directly. Life, deeds, and words come together, and if they match, the church becomes a powerful witness of God's grace and reconciliation, love and renewal. The local church cannot not witness in public. Its presence will speak loudly – positively or negatively. It will attract people to the kingdom or distract them from it. The church should be aware of this and consciously accept its ecclesial position and responsibility for the community. This is the only way to become a positive agent of God to the people.

Whether a church is faithful to God's missionary commission will be seen in how it relates to its neighbours. Do people see God's light in it; do they feel loved, and experience it as an advocate for the needy? Then they will cherish its presence in the neighbourhood even when they themselves may follow different religious and ideological convictions. A church in community, caring for the well-being of the people, involved in community development – such a church becomes a people's church. And a people's church is always politically relevant.

A church may test its relevancy for the community by the simple question of whether it is needed locally. What would people miss if your church one day ceased to exist? Would somebody notice its absence? Would the kindergarten, the school, the social department of the city, the media, miss you? If so, your church proves it is relevant to society, politically active, and transformative. If not, your church has stopped being salt and light for your community, meaning it has lost its missionary vision and is hardly any longer the church of Christ, the *ecclesia* of God. A church which does not follow its missionary call and does not embody the gospel has lost its nature and represents a religious club rather than a people of God. And as such it will be less and less attractive to people. Its voice will stay unheard and its proclamation become an empty calling to an irrelevant religion. Political engagement of the church in the frame described above goes hand-in-hand with its evangelistic effectiveness.

6.6. The Alternative Society

The church of Christ is his *ecclesia* in the midst of a world not yet reconciled with God. It is his priest, royal servant, and prophetic voice. All its public action is highly political. But the most political expression is its very being – that of a new society of the kingdom of God in the midst of human kingdoms. It is God's alternative social space. In it, humans see a different way of living, a new culture, a positive alternative to what is ruling their lives. Members of the church do not only accept the cultural mandate given to all humans by God; they do not only engage in societal transformation on all levels of life; they engage in much more – in discipling the nation, introducing the ethics of Jesus as a godly way of life. This is the essence of the Great Commission in Matthew 28:19–20.

No wonder the high moral standard of living among Christians is, especially in Western societies, under threat. The autonomous human does not want to submit under the authority of God. The active presence of the church in society hinders human autonomy and is a basic reason for the societal powers pushing the church out of the public square into the private sphere. A missional church will never allow this to happen. Not even under threat to life.

The church as an alternative community is a political reality par excellence. Therefore, a politically active church will consciously engage in church planting. Where there is no church in community, an ecclesial transformation of the community is literally impossible. Transformation requires an agent of transformation, and a local transformation of community – a local agent. *Missio politica* of the church must, therefore, include a mission of planting churches. Separating socio-political engagement of the church from evangelism and church planting leads to a major reduction in success of God's mission in the world.

The forces behind such a separation are in no way interested in seeing the kingdom of God grow. On the contrary, they may invite the church to turn stones into bread in order to feed the hungry masses, but always at the expense of falling down before the anti-godly, demonic presence. Jesus, who was tempted by Satan in the beginning of his ministry to do exactly this, clearly rejected such an option identifying the true face of Satan behind the offer (Matt 4:1–4). He did feed the hungry, he did heal the sick, but never without letting those know where his power came from. The *missio politica* is integral and wholistic in the best sense of the word.

Planting kingdom communities in the world with a commission to become communal priests and royal servants with a bold voice in favour of those who long for justice and righteousness is what Jesus aimed for by sending his disciples to the ends of the world.

7

Missio Politica – a Mission of Peace

7.1. Men and Women of Peace

As Christians we are invited to follow God in all of his mission on earth. Where he is, we shall be also. To discover him among the nations means we find the right point of departure for our own mission, and to discover those men and women he is working with will open doors for us for effective missional ministries in the public. In recent years the term Church-Planting-Movement (CPM) as promoted by David Garrison[1] and David Watson,[2] claiming amazing results all over the world, has shaken the church-planting scene in the West. I will not comment on the movement as such. What I will do, though, is use one of the central terms of CPM – the idea of the *person of peace*.

According to Watson, missionaries and church planters have to contact the right person in the target community in order to establish a meaningful relationship to the community they want to evangelize. Watson defines the person of peace as follows: "The Person of Peace is the one God has prepared to receive the gospel for the first time into a community."[3] Watson derives his idea from Jesus commanding his disciples to go and proclaim the gospel to

---

1. David Garrisson, *Church Planting Movements* (Richmond, VA: Office of Overseas Operations, International Mission Board of the Southern Baptist Convention, 2004). https://de.scribd.com/document/73786524/David-Garrison-CPM-Booklet (Last access: 23 August 2017).

2. See for instance David Watson and Paul Watson, *Contagious Disciple Making: Leading Others on a Journey of Discovery* (Nashville, TN: Thomas Nelson, 2014).

3. http://www.davidlwatson.org/2008/02/14/church-planting-essentials---find-the-person-of-peace/ (Last access: 1 June 2015).

the lost sheep of the house of Israel by entering the houses of the people in Matthew 10 and Luke 10. He commands his disciples to find a person of peace and stay in this house. In Luke 10:6 we read (in a slightly modified form): "When you enter a house offer peace. If a person of peace is present then stay in the house, eat and drink what is put before you, and do not move around from house to house."

The principle is widely applied, for instance, in house church movements, as Victor Chodhrie reports for his Indian context.[4] CPM promoters build on peace found by the disciples and missionaries in the house of the non-Christian. Here they find a key to the whole of the community. Leading the "person of peace" to Christ will give them both an open door to the community and an interpreter to help them find the right language and the right form of communication for the people. Entering the community with such indigenes and well-informed assistance guarantees proper contextualization and the right cultural expression of the church to be built. It is most definitely a valid and powerful concept.

What the CPM promoters emphasize less is the fact that in the biblical passage used to justify the concept, Jesus commands his disciples to *offer* peace. They are the people of peace coming into a house in which peace is welcomed. In other words their mission is a mission of peace. A person of peace in the house that the disciples enter accepts peace, welcomes the ambassadors of peace, and becomes therefore both the contact person to the community in which peace is needed and the place where God's peace will be transported. The missional involvement of the church in society is first and foremost an action of peace. Peacemaking is the core of all political mission of the church.

7.2. Mission, Violence, and Peace

Jesus sent his disciples "to offer peace" (Luke 10:6). He the peacemaker grants his disciples peace to become missionaries in accordance with his own calling (John 20:21). He came to the world to introduce to the world the good year of the Lord, the Jubilee year, which included the restoration of shalom in personal, social, and even ecological terms. In Luke 4:18–19 we read: "The Spirit of the Lord is on me, because he has anointed me to proclaim good news to the poor. He has sent me to proclaim freedom for the prisoners and recovery of sight for

---

4. Victor Chodhrie, "The Training of House Church Leaders," in *Nexus: The World House Church Reader,* ed. by Rad Zdero (Pasadena, CA: WCL, 2007), 44.

the blind, to set the oppressed free, to proclaim the year of the Lord's favour."
The message is clear: Jesus came to bring shalom, the all-encompassing peace
to his people, the ultimate state of peace inwardly and outwardly. The apostle
Paul, who followed Jesus in his theology and practice, expresses this in his
epistle to the Ephesians in the following words:

> For he himself is our peace, who has made the two groups one and
> has destroyed the barrier, the dividing wall of hostility, by setting
> aside in his flesh the law with its commands and regulations. His
> purpose was to create in himself one new humanity out of the two,
> thus making peace, and in one body to reconcile both of them to
> God through the cross, by which he put to death their hostility.
> He came and preached peace to you who were far away and peace
> to those who were near. For through him we both have access to
> the Father by one Spirit.
>
> Consequently, you are no longer foreigners and strangers,
> but fellow citizens with God's people and also members of his
> household. (Eph 2:14–20)

The mission of Jesus is shalomic in nature.

Disciples of Christ are sent to "offer peace." They are sent as Jesus was sent
(John 20:21) to bring peace to those who are near and those afar. Their mission
is qualified by what Jesus did in reconciling the world in conflict with God
himself (2 Cor 5:18–20). He is the prince of peace (Isa 9:6). To discuss Christian
mission and avoid the issue of violence and peace is literally impossible. It is
rather strange that evangelical missiology has not dealt much with the question
of violence and peace. They seem to concentrate on the inward peace, the
reconciliation between God and men. Conflicts between people, violence,
and discomfort in societies are rather left out as if it would not be a matter of
God's commission. There are, of course, books and articles on mission history
pointing to the violent history of Christian mission, for example in the Patristic
or Middle Ages.[5] Few missiologies reflect on mission as a peace witness.

---

5. See for instance, David J. Bosch, *Transforming Mission: Pradigm Shifts in Theology of
Mission* (Maryknoll, NY: Orbis, 1991), 108–113, 222–226. Alan Kreider, "Mission and Violence:
Inculturation in the Fourth Century – Basil and Ambrose," in *Mission in Context: Explorations
Inspired by J. Andrew Kirk*, ed. by John Corrie and Kathy Ross (Farnham, Surrey: Ashgate,
2012), 201–216.

It is our task to recover theologically the importance of Christian peace witness and missionary engagement for peace.[6] Christian mission must return to what the *missio Dei*, the mission of God requires. Any reduction of God's mission is not only problematic; it will amount to a complete failure of the mission of the church. The historical examples for this are many.[7] We have to recover the theological foundation of our mission as peace building and the character of a missionary as a peace builder. For the first part I will point us to the rich literature on the issue produced by the peace-church tradition, in particular by John Howard Yoder of the Mennonite Church,[8] and the discussion of this position.[9] Our subject here is the person and ministry of the peace-bearing missionary.

7.3. A Person of Peace Promotes Peace

Our Christian mission started with the resurrected Christ appearing in front of his disciples. In John 20:19–23 we read:

> On the evening of that first day of the week, when the disciples were together, with the doors locked for fear of the Jewish leaders, Jesus came and stood among them and said, "Peace be with you!" After he said this, he showed them his hands and side. The disciples were overjoyed when they saw the Lord.
>
> Again Jesus said, "Peace be with you! As the Father has sent me, I am sending you." And with that he breathed on them and said, "Receive the Holy Spirit. If you forgive anyone's sins, their sins are forgiven; if you do not forgive them, they are not forgiven."

The resurrected Christ grants his disciples his peace and his spirit before he sends them as the "father has sent him." Here we find the two conditions which determine the Christian missionary as peace builder: they (a) receive the peace of the Lord, and (b) are filled with the Holy Spirit.

---

6. See in this regard Robert L. Ramseyer, ed. *Mission and the Peace Witness: The Gospel and Christian Discipleship* (Scottdale: Herald Press, 1979).

7. David J. Bosch in his great volume on mission through the ages points to the paradigm changes following a reduced vision of what mission in a certain period was meant to be (Bosch, *Transforming Mission*).

8. See for instance, Yoder's classics: *The Politics of Jesus* (Grand Rapids, MI: Eerdmans, 1972); *The Original Revolution: Essays on Christian Pacifism* (Scottdale: Herald Press, 1972); *The Priestly Kingdom: Social Ethics as Gospel* (Notre Dame: University of Notre Dame Press, 1984).

9. J. Andrew Kirk, *Mission under Scrutiny: Confronting Current Challenge* (London: Darton, Longman & Todd, 2006), 133–150.

First the missionaries have received the peace of the Lord. Only peaceful people will lead others to peace. And peacefulness means personal conflicts are resolved, hatred is no longer super-impressed but truly removed. Research shows that most missionaries returning home after failing on the mission field did not develop their problems in the mission – they brought them along when they went into mission.[10] In fact many missionaries go into mission hoping finally to resolve their inner conflicts by fully dedicating their life to Jesus. But things do not work like that. Nobody will ever follow Jesus properly without becoming born again. To Nicodemus Jesus said, "Very truly I tell you, no one can see the kingdom of God unless they are born again" (John 3:3). Renewed people will enter a ministry of renewal and restoration. Whenever Jesus renews and restores people he does so in a complete manner. He promised to give peace to his disciples of a quality that the world cannot give. In John 14:27 Jesus says, "Peace I leave with you; my peace I give you. I do not give to you as the world gives. Do not let your hearts be troubled and do not be afraid."

Let me illustrate the power of peace given by Jesus using my own example. I grew up in the former Soviet Union. I became a Christian through a miraculous intervention of Jesus and joined an evangelical church that followed a strict pacifistic theology of non-violence. When the time came to join the military, I decided not to take up arms. This resulted in imprisonment and harsh times for me. One little story changed my whole life. Before becoming a Christian I used to box and the Soviets knew this, of course. One day I was called into the office of a secret police officer. He read to me Matthew 5:39 where Jesus says, "But I tell you, do not resist an evil person. If anyone slaps you on the right cheek, turn to them the other cheek also." He asked me whether I believed this, what he called nonsense. I confirmed that I did believe it. Then he called a Muslim boy in and forced him to hit one of my teeth out. This was repeated many nights. Many of my teeth were gone. "Just say you do not believe the Jesus words any longer," the officer promised, "and we will stop the torture." I used to be a boxer; it was not the pain or the missing teeth, but it was my absolute helplessness in the situation that started to fill my heart with hatred. Honestly, if I could have, I would have killed both of them. This hatred worried me most. So I went to the Lord, crying tears, and asking him to grant me his peace of mind. Then the Spirit of God fell into my body with such a might, I was unable to stay on my feet any longer, and with him indescribable peace

---

10. Marion Knell, *Families on the Move: Growing Up Overseas – and Loving it!* (Grand Rapids, MI: Monarch Books, 2001), 48.

and love for my torturers filled my soul. The hate was gone. Peace and love were there. For the first time in my life I felt like I was ready to let my life go for Jesus's sake. And since then, I have been a changed man.[11]

Second, the missionaries of peace are filled with the Holy Spirit. Jesus himself grants his disciples the Holy Spirit, and commends them not to leave Jerusalem, not to attempt any ministry until the Spirit of God comes and empowers them (Acts 1:8). In fact, his coming to earth marks the start of the church and its mission. This is obviously true for our mission of mediation and peace as well.

You can see how this functioned in the early church in Jerusalem. Remember the first conflict in the young family of the followers of Jesus. The Greek-speaking widows in the church had been overlooked. There is conflict in the air. The apostles have to solve the problem immediately, and they solve it by appointing deacons in charge of food distribution, men full of wisdom and the Spirit of God (Acts 6:3). Conflict resolution, acts and deeds of peace, require the presence of the Holy Spirit. It is not enough to understand the issues involved in violence and conflict, and it is not enough to receive training in conflict resolution. This might all be very helpful, but the Christian peace mission is Spirit guided. He is the Lord of mission (2 Cor 3:17), and our peace mission is no exemption.

This is where the power of Christian conflict resolution and peace building comes from. Jesus promises to send his Spirit who will come and convince the world of their sin, his righteousness, and the judgment, and will lead people into all truth (John 16:8–12). This is the condition of peace building; peace can only be established when the conflicting parties recognize their failure, their sin, and when they understand the consequences and the futility of living in conflict and see the whole and true picture. In their guiding principles, the Life and Peace Institute in Uppsala, Sweden, names principles which include knowledge of the people, local conditions, traditions, and of course, the nature of conflicts.[12] Recognition of sin, judgment, and truth is central to all conflict resolution. And truth "integrates all dimensions of the human world – intellectual, spiritual, emotional, academic and ethical. . . . Truth, by its very nature, covers the whole of life."[13] According to Jesus, this is what the Spirit of God will do in the life of people who come near to him.

---

11. See the whole story in Johannes Reimer, *Liberty in Confinement: A Story of Faith in the Red Army* (Winnipeg: Kindred Press, 2000).

12. http://life-peace.org/approach/guiding-principles-2/ (Last access: 1 June 2015).

13. J. Andrew Kirk, *Mission under Scrutiny,* 133.

Peacemakers will be strongly advised to follow the guidance of the Spirit. Filled with the Spirit they will come up with words of revelation and wisdom, identifying the real powers behind the conflict, because the Spirit grants them his gift to discern the spirits. All these qualities are gifts of the Spirit (1 Cor 12:8–31). Whenever they miss some of those gifts, there are sisters and brothers in Christ gifted and prepared to come along. The mission of peace is a task given to the whole body of Christ, and this body represents "the fullness of all in all" (Eph 1:23). There will never be anything this body will miss if the parts obey and follow their master missionary – the Holy Spirit.

7.4. Peacemaking – the Heart of God's Mission

Mission brings peace into the world. "Overcoming violence and building peace" is clearly an important dimension of our Christian mission.[14] Christian mission can never engage in violence; overcoming violence with violence is never an option for Christian mission.[15] The church of Christ is God's prophetic voice, and it is a voice of peace. The church of Christ is God's ambassador of reconciliation. It must engage in peace building. Its peace witness is at the heart of its calling.[16] Whenever Christians worked for and proclaimed peace in history, the church expanded and the kingdom of God grew. Its peace engagement was never easy, and more than once Christians paid a high price for their refusal to join the violent or to use violence for the sake of the kingdom. But even where Christians died, their blood became a seed for revival, restoration, and the kingdom.

On the other hand, where the church engaged in violence, it lost its territory to other forces; consider the Middle East and North Africa. Peacemaking is God's way of creating space where he meets people, reconciling them with himself and with one another. Even today there are a number of impressive examples of Christian peacemaking engagements – in violent Somalia, for

---

14. J. Andrew Kirk, *What Is Mission? Theological Explorations* (London: Darton, Longman & Todd, 1999), 143–163.

15. See in this regard the discussion in J. Andrew Kirk, *Mission under Scrutiny*, 133–150.

16. See in this regard Stephen B. Bevans and Roger P. Schroeder's appeal in *Constants in Context: A Theology of Mission for Today* (Maryknoll, NY: Orbis 2004), 273–275.

instance,[17] or in South Africa, in Nepal,[18] Rwanda, and Burundi, just to mention some.

7.5. Peacemaking in Context

We turn back to the opening words of this chapter. Jesus sends his disciples on a mission of peace, and he encourages them to find a person of peace in a town they enter to bring peace. He determines mission as an act *with the people* rather than *for the people.* The peace-minded in the world are the point of departure for our Christian peacemaking. They are the key to the local people; they understand the nature of the local conflict; they speak the language and understand the culture. The missionary might facilitate a process, but the local people will need to play a central role in that process. Even when they might not yet follow Jesus, they follow his heart of peace. The local person of peace is central to the idea of mission as Jesus presents it.

The people of peace are God's chosen. It will not take long, and they may soon understand that their heart's desire springs from God's grace given to them one way or another. Mission with the people is what the CPM has discovered, but it should be generally the approach for all mission in the world. Especially where peacemaking is involved. Peacemaking is always a process, which involves those in need of peace and those who know peace. Peacemaking is a community event. It enters community in conflict and builds a community of peace.

There is one more truth in the biblical narrative: the disciples are asked to enter the house of the person of peace and stay there. The house represents the means to be used by the disciples on their missionary journey. Here they find support, food, and even a meeting place for the actions to be taken. All of this is not on their own. Jesus commands them to use local means to accomplish their mission.

This, it seems to me, is a crucial point for all Christian mission. It is not what we bring to the people that decides the success or failure but what we find among the people themselves. Western mission comes with a sponsor

---

17. Wolfgang Heinrich, *Building the Peace: Experiences of Collaborative Peace-Building in Somalia 1993–1996* (Uppsala: Life & Peace Institute, 1997); Thamia Paffenholz, *Community Based Bottom-up Peace-Building* (Uppsala: Life & Peace Institute, 2003), for example.

18. *Learning from Other Peace Processes,* by John Paul Lederach, John Darby, Madhav Joshi, in *Republica,* May 3–5/2011. Digital in: http://www.myrepublica.com/portal/index.php?action=news_details&news_id=30843 (Last access: 1 June 2015).

mentality. All the best methodology of mission in general and peacemaking in particular is designed in the West. The West gives its best, only to find out that the Western means do not necessarily work in different cultures. Just look at Iraq and the results left behind from a Western attempt to bring peace and democracy to a country under Muslim dictatorship. Things are worse today than ever before. Or look at Libya: Western intervention with all its arrogance of being better is less helpful because it claims truth where ideology has flooded society, even in mission agencies. It is the local culture and the local framework of life that first and foremost should be used to promote mission. A person of peace is not only a partner for the Christian peace mission – she or he offers the language, the cultural framework, and methodology. They are God's keys to communities. They know their own people, see their needs, and engage for the better. They sense injustice and some even offer their lives fighting for justice and transformation. Perhaps they may not know Jesus yet, but God knows them and prepares them for a ministry of his kingdom. We do well to join hands with them in community development and work together for the better of life around us. We will learn to trust each other by establishing a working convivial space.

Our togetherness will not, however, downplay the ethical and spiritual differences among us; to the contrary, it will encourage us to talk them through, to debate and even fight in an ongoing discourse for the truth of the gospel. Friends and partners in social and community development will become critical dialogue partners striving for an appropriate change of mind and heart. As Christians we will always stay obedient to the missionary call of Jesus to make disciples of him.

8

The Politics of the Church – Moving into the Public Square

8.1. The Point of Departure

The church has a political mandate; the mission of God is always political. Being involved in the mission of God means being involved in wholistic transformation and is by definition political. The question is, however, how does the church approach its political mandate? What are the crucial markers for its meaningful involvement in the public square? These are questions many churches ask, for instance, The Good Hope Church in one of our German cities: "We understand our mission, Johannes," explained the pastor of the church about his dilemma, "but what would a meaningful involvement of our church in the city be? Where are the chances and challenges, and where are limits to our involvement? We do pray for the city, but our prayer is seldom concrete, and I suppose it is because we are not really involved with the people."

I am hearing the question of the pastor of Good Hope everywhere in the world. Are there criteria which help us to decide what is right, what is wrong? To do so, we have to understand how the world we are living in functions. You only transform what you understand. The politically involved church needs a theology of the world to rightly determine its involvement.

What do we have to know about the world in order to enable us to act responsibly? Two basic insights will be crucially important for the missionary praxis of the church in the public square: (a) a theological view of the world and (b) an anthropological model of the world.

8.1.1. The Tripolar World

A comprehensive and biblical vision of the world realizes that the world around us must be seen as tripolar. It is on the one hand God's created world. There is nothing wrong in what he made. The apostle Paul even claims that in creation people may see God's nature and adore him (Rom 1). On the other hand the world is also a product of human civilizing genius. Commissioned by God (Gen 1:27–28) men and women have created great cultures and civilizations all around the world, and not all of it is bad. Some of what people have made is astoundingly great. Just consider our own time and all the technology we use. But there is a third power in the world – Satan and his demons, who destroy all life, corrupt all good beginnings.

Let me illustrate what I mean by using the example of world religions. In the past things were very simple. We drew a clear line between Christianity, the only right religion, and the other non-Christian religions. Hendrik Kraemer, for instance, strictly declared all non-Christian religions as demonic.[1] Today we understand that such a view is oversimplified and hold with the German missiologist, Peter Beyerhaus, a more comprehensive, three-polar view of religion, discovering in the other faiths God's presence, human creativity, and of course, demonic deception.[2] All people seek for an explanation of the unknown, long to receive answers to their questions about the transcendent, and even experience the greatness of the Creator. You will find traces of God in all world religions. Beyerhaus calls this the theonomic principle. Others have preferred to use the term general revelation.[3]

On the other hand, humans have developed their own religious ideas. Coping with the unknown, they gave names to the phenomena, designed religious theories, established rites and rituals, moral values and ethical principles. Religion, Theo Sundermeier states, is always "a joint answer of people to the transcendental experience in rite and ethic."[4] And, as with all

---

1. Hendrick Kraemer, *The Christian Message in a Non-Christian World,* reprint in Missiological Classics Series, Vol. 6, ed. by Siga Arles (Bangalore: Center for Contemporary Christianity, 2009), 101ff. Kraemer's position is critically discussed against his biography and the context of his time in Carl F. Hallencreutz, *Kraemer towards Tambaram: A Study in Hendrik Kraemer's Missionary Approach* (Uppsala: Almquist & Wiksells, 1996).

2. Peter Beyerhaus, "Zur Theologie der Religionen im Protestantismus," *Kerygma und Dogma* 15 (1969): 100–104.

3. See the discussion in Bruce A. Demarest, *General Revelation: Historical Views and Contemporary Issues* (Grand Rapids: Zondervan, 1982).

4. Theo Sundermeier, *Was ist Religion? Religionswissenschaft im Theologischen Kontext* (Gütersloh: Gütersloher Verlagshaus, 1999), 27.

human invention, such an answer is never absolute, never totally wrong or totally right. It is contextual, preliminary, and subjective.

Third, says Beyerhaus, religions are demonically influenced, deceived, and corrupted. Satan will always try to mislead humans and estrange them from God. In conclusion, religions are complex realities. There can never be a simple dividing line of wrong and right in the phenomena, not to mention the adherents. It is not wise to call God's presence among them wrong or eliminate creative human thinking, but of course, it would be complete nonsense to accept the demonic. We do well to distinguish, to be critical, and at the same time open to discover the unexpected presence of the Most High in the midst of even a non-biblical religion. The world around us requires a comprehensive approach. Simplistic theological ideas are dangerous. Mission here is a journey to and with the people, following God's presence among them in a constant battle with the enemy. God's general presence in the world leads us to consider inclusiveness as a vital category of missional praxis. The human genius will force us to think about cooperation, and the reality of the evil in the world forces us to consider entering a battle. What does this mean in practical terms?

8.1.2. The Four Level Culture

We are called to go and disciple the *ethne*, the nations (Matt 28:18–20). The Greek term *ethnos,* as we have said above, stands for a socio-political space. The best translation today simply is culture – understood as "a way of life of a given people" or "design for living," as Lothar Käser suggested.[5] To disciple nations means to transform the socio-political reality of the *ethnos* according to the teachings of Jesus. To do this, we have to understand culture structurally. Herbert Kane has noted: "Understanding the culture can *spell* the difference between success and failure in introducing new ideas or methods . . . the missionary . . . should also have all the knowledge that is available about the nature of human society and culture before he begins to administer new ideas, which constitute the medicine of social change."[6] And Dennis Teague in his very inspiring book on the correlation between culture and mission underlines the importance of cultural understanding as "essential to church growth."[7]

---

5. Lothar Käser, *Fremde Kulturen, Eine Einführung in die Ethnologie* (Bad Liebenzell: VLM, 1999), 37.

6. Herbert Kane, *Wanted: World Christians* (Grand Rapids, MI: Baker, 1986), 64; see also Dennis Teague, *Culture – the Missing Link in Missions* (Manila: OMF Literature, 1996), 159.

7. Teague, *Culture,* 166.

Culture as "a way of living" is, according to cultural anthropology, multi-dimensional.[8] Gary Ferraro is right when he divides the cultural space into four levels: (a) things we have or the material culture; (b) things we do or the social culture; (c) things we think or the cognitive culture and, last (d) things we believe or the religious culture. We could also speak of religion, worldview, social set of values, and material-achieving.

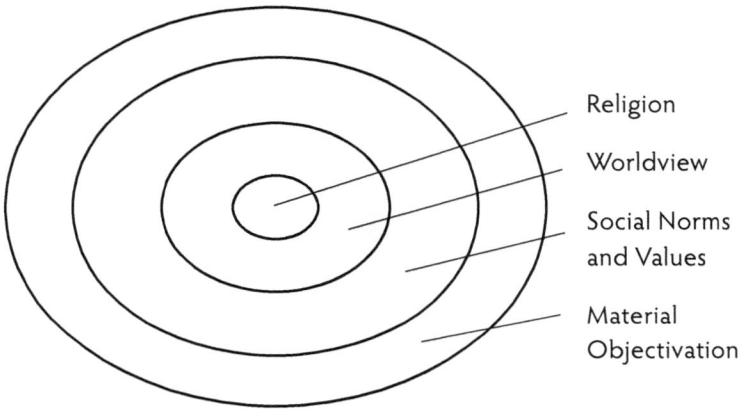

Religion

Worldview

Social Norms and Values

Material Objectivation

Cultural Dimensions

According to anthropological research, what we believe informs our thinking, what we think informs our behaviour, and what we do informs our material status. We have what we do, we do what we think, and we think what we believe. In our chart the power of influence runs from the centre to the periphery. This is why it is so important to change the faith of the people. Right beliefs will care for proper worldviews and determine right behaviour and physical involvement. Renewal, says the apostle Paul, requires a change of mind (Rom 12:1–2).

But how do you get there? How do we reach the mind and the belief system of the people? Here too, insights from cultural anthropology are most helpful. Anthropological studies show that any cultural change starts from the periphery and works itself to the centre because changes are challenges. To apply change you will have to win trust with the people and trust does not

---

8. Gary Ferraro, *Cultural Anthropology: An Applied Perspective* (Independence: Wadsworth, 1998), 18; Stephen Dahl, "Einführung in die Interkulturelle Kommunikation," online http://www.intercultural-network.de/einführung (Last accessed: 19 June 2013), 4.

develop through debates and discussions. It is when you work together for the common good, when you talk and discuss together about your common needs in individual and community matters – then you develop trust. And only when basic trust is established, change might be possible, because change will always challenge traditional thinking and beliefs. Debates and battles over right and wrong, risk and potential failure, are unavoidable. Most change initiatives lose their potential and dynamics right at this point.

This is not much different in the area of mission. Marvin Meyers speaks of the Question of Prior Trust (QPT) as the basic precondition for any communication of the gospel.[9] People will not listen to us, and they will obviously not agree to change their ways of living without trusting us to guide them to the best message of the world. Again trust is not won by entering a religious debate but by involving ourselves in community transformation, by working side by side with the people.

In other words, living and working with people in developing a common space of living, discussing felt needs, and searching together for ways of solving them creates ties of trust, a togetherness which holds strong even in times of debate, stress, and questioning of traditional systems of worldview and belief.

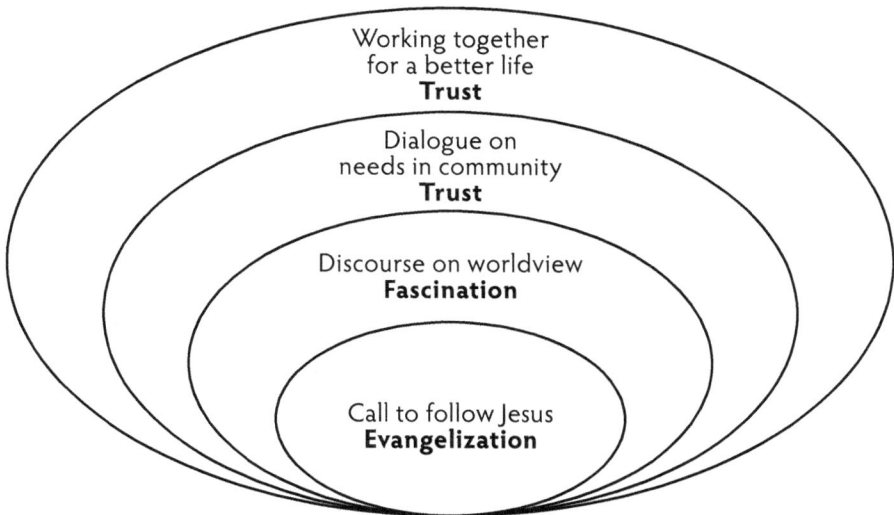

Process of Communal Transformation

---

9. Marvin K. Meyers, *Christianity Confronts Culture* (Grand Rapids: Zondervan, 1981), 32f.

8.2. God in the World – Join Him

Christian mission takes place in the world. It is the world God aims to reconcile to himself in Jesus Christ (2 Cor 5:18). He is the first missionary. Mission is his idea and his work,[10] his heart-piece.[11] Whoever enters the world of mission will have to join God in his mission. God is always first. He is always present, even among those who live rebellious lives. He is the life factor in the world, its sustainer. Take him out, and the world will collapse.

The church involved in political mission will have to join God in his mission in the world. He is the determining factor in all mission. The church will only participate in what he does. But in order to do so, it has to sharpen its vision and discover God in action. We only join when we know where and what. Few churches have asked the question where is God in their community. What missionary and political emphasis does he set? To his disciples Jesus once said that at the end of time judgment will concentrate on questions of social involvement. In Matthew 25 we read that it is important to know where God is in our city.

And how do we know? Who tells us where God is at the moment? Remember Jesus. He was still a child when he travelled with his parents to Jerusalem and his parents lost sight of him. When after days of intensive searching they finally found him, his mother, Mary, was a bit upset with her son. And Jesus? What did he reply?

It seems so easy. Know the heart of your son and you will soon find him where he belongs. Know the heart of God, and it will not be difficult to know where he is. The just God will be where people cry for justice; the righteous Lord will stay with those in need of righteousness. God will be where the needy meet and the oppressed cry their tears and the sick search for a healer. Knowing God's heart, we soon discover him in action.

The church may just ask him. He obviously hears the voice of those who want to join him, opens the door when we knock and ask for permission to enter (Matt 7:7). Surely this presupposes a personal relationship with God, but isn't the Spirit of God sent to us to accomplish exactly that? He came to lead the disciples of Christ into all truth. Ask him!

The Hope Church I mentioned above had to learn this first basic lesson. As the church we follow God in his participation in the world. We connect to

---

10. Georg Vicedom, *Missio Dei: Einführung in eine Theologie der Mission,* ed. Klaus W. Müller. Edition afem, Mission Classics, Vol. 4 (Nürnberg: VTR, 2002), 32.

11. Escobar, *La Palabra,* 86.

him. We aim towards his kingdom, his rule. He sets the agenda; he determines the means and methods and takes the lead for every missionary step we take in public. The day they understood that, things changed. The pastor states:

> We discover God in so many places in our city today. We started to prayer-walk the city. Once a month we do it. We ask him to lead us to places where he is active, and needless to say, he showed us those places. He is with the refugees, the unemployed, the street people without a shelter, and many, many others in the city. We have been led to broken business-people, depressed politicians, school teachers, psychologists, and so on and so on. Joining God has become a blessing to all of us. It is easy to work hard when you know God himself is in the midst of it.

The political mission of the church is first of all marked by its connection to God in action. It will do its priestly, royal, and prophetic ministry well when it accepts the leadership of God the Spirit and does the works Jesus did.

8.3. People of the World – Partner with Them

God does his mission in the world among people. In fact humans are made in his own image. They are chosen to rule and cultivate the world (Gen 1:27–28). To join God in mission means to understand and accept humanity as the most crucial point of departure for God's mission in the world.

It is widely accepted in missiological circles that mission requires involvement, contextualization, and inculturation. You cannot reach people with the gospel without learning their language, rituals and rules, values, and other religious and cultural settings. Only when we understand the people will we start to communicate meaningfully with them, so that they may understand what we have in mind. Mission of the church is for the people, and the church is "a community for the world,"[12] or as Dietrich Bonhoeffer puts it, "The church is the church only when it exists for others . . . The church must share in the secular problems of ordinary human life, not dominating, but helping and serving."[13]

But how do we find in-roads into a foreign culture? How do we become such a *church for others*, without falling into the helper syndrome of "pro-

---

12. Karl Barth, *Church Dogmatics IV/3* (Edinburgh: T&T Clark, 1962), 762ff.
13. Dietrich Bonhoeffer, *Letters and Papers from Prison,* enlarged ed. (London: SCM, 1971), 382f.

existence" as the German missiologist Theo Sundermeier, reflecting on Bonhoeffer's phrase and its liberal-humanist background, critically observes.[14] Too often the *church for others* knew better what the others needed, and the helper soon dominated those in need of help. Political transformation turned into political domination. Sundermeier, therefore, suggested, instead of talking about a church *for others,* we should speak of the church *with* others.[15] No pro-existence is required in mission but rather co-existence.[16]

Similarly, Gourdet suggests that identification with the people can only be reached through realistic participation in the life of the people, which requires less that we work for the people but rather work with them.[17] Without being close to the people we will not be able to develop proper ways of missionary communication, because we will not be able to learn from and with them.[18] And learning together with those whom we seek to transform is a crucial precondition for any meaningful mission, including political.[19]

Transformation requires an open space in which all participants in the process are welcomed to share their part of the story without limits. Such an open space presupposes a culture of welcome,[20] and a culture of welcome in turn presupposes clarity regarding the aim and means of mission.

Here is our second marker of proper political involvement of the church – it is done as mission with the people in a participatory manner, serving and never dominating. Our Hope Church had to learn this basic lesson. Discovering God in the marketplace, they started to share, serve, and minister to the people. The needy thankfully accepted their gifts, but failed to join God and the church. Surprised by such a turn, the pastor asked for advice. I remember asking him: "Do you think people enjoy a Santa Claus?" "Sure, everybody loves the Santa and his presents," he replied. "But do they join him in daily life?" I continued to ask him. He immediately agreed: serving people by being a Santa Claus

---

14. Theo Sundermeier, "Konvivenz als Grundstruktur ökumenischer Existenz heute," in *Ökumenische Existenz Heute* 1 (1986): 62ff. See also David J. Bosch, *Transforming Mission,* 384.

15. Sundermeier.

16. Sundermeier, *Konvivenz,* 65.

17. S. Gourdet, "Identification in Intercultural Communication," *Missionalia* 24 (March 1996): 407f.

18. David J. Hesselgrave, *Communicating Christ Cross-Culturally: An Introduction to Missionary Communication* (Grand Rapids: Zondervan, 1991), 46.

19. Jacob Loewen, *Culture and Human Values: Christian Interpretation in Anthropological Perspective* (Pasadena, CA: WCL, 1977), 36. See also Gourdet, *Identification,* 407; Paul G. Hiebert, *Anthropological Insights for Missionaries* (Grand Rapids: Baker, 1985), 81f.

20. See more about the concept of participation in a culture of welcome in Johannes Reimer, *Hereinspaziert: Willkommenskultur und Evangelisation* (Schwarzenfeld: Neufeld, 2013), 140ff.

does not give people dignity, in fact it makes them beggars, dependent, even weaker than they were before they got to know the Christians. "What do we do then?" the pastor asked me. This is the point where I introduced to him the four levels of culture and explained to him how change in a culture works. "You start with serving together, talking together, fighting for the right solution together. This is the way to establish trust, and without trust there will be no real willingness to change." And the church changed. First they joined already existing community development projects, and then they even initiated their own projects, always together with the community. For the apostle Paul, becoming a Jew to the Jews, a Gentile to the Gentiles was the way to reach out to people. As Jesus before him, he wanted to immerse himself among the people, live with and for them, and then win some for the glory of God as he experienced it. The Hope Church discovered a similar pattern.

The theory of change as it is expressed in terms of cultural anthropology works only inclusively. Only when you stay with the people, work alongside the people, dialogue and debate with them may you introduce change.

This is cultural anthropology, you may say, a theory of intercultural communication. Christian mission, however, derives from biblical grounds. It is not enough to claim working with the unbelieving as a trust-building venture on the grounds of what cultural anthropology teaches. Where does the Bible suggest working together with sinners in order to free them from their bondage? Is there biblical evidence for a mission-with-others?

The answer is twofold: (a) we have to consider the lasting validity of the cultural mandate given to all humanity; (b) we orientate ourselves on Jesus, the prime source and agent of mission and evangelism.

First, we have suggested that we start our mission by engaging in the material and social transformation of a community with the people of the community. By using tools of community development, we may establish trust with the people, which may lead to a deeper level of mission and evangelism. The mandate for doing this together we find in Genesis 1:27–28, in the so-called cultural mandate.[21] Here God commissions humans to cultivate the land and rule over the earth. His commission has never been taken back. George Peters states, "It is man's responsibility to build a wholesome culture in which man can live as a true human being according to the moral order and creative purposes of God."[22] It is still valid for all the people. And the best

---

21. The term has been broadly discussed by George W. Peters, *A Biblical Theology*, 166f.
22. Peters.

evidence for this is the cultures and societies themselves developed by humans. Just look around you. Some Japanese Buddhist may not yet know Jesus, but they understand the validity of culture and meaningful societal structures. The most impressive cultural achievements are found in Confucian China, and the first humans conquering space were communist Russians. Religious orientation has not prevented humans from being culturally active. The apostle Paul says, "The authorities that exist have been established by God" (Rom 13:1). We work together with the people for a better life because this is clearly the will of God, and his will is expressed in his cultural mandate. All humans, regardless of whether they follow Jesus or not, are subject to this mandate. It is not only possible to work together with others on material and social issues in community development, it is our duty.

Second, we orientate our mission on Jesus. His life began with a surprise. Not the spiritual leaders of Israel, but rather Gentile magicians from the East were the first to notice his divine birth. And later in ministry, he, the one who is sent to the lost sheep of this God-chosen nation, avoided connecting to the religious elite; instead he called fishermen, tax collectors, or even a less-than-perfect woman to become his disciples. The religious elite observed his ways of engaging the community and blamed him for eating and drinking with sinners (Luke 19:7). His willingness to discover the potential of a faith community goes far beyond Israel. He praises a Roman soldier for his faith and uses a Samaritan as an example of love and care for the needy (Luke 10:25–37). In fact, the expression "Good Samaritan" has become a basic term for care. Jesus engages in a conversation with a prostitute woman, and the whole Samaritan city of Sichar runs out to see him (John 4:1–42). He commands his disciples to feed a crowd of five thousand men, knowing that the only food, the five loaves of bread and two fish, will be found in the basket of a little boy who did not belong to his followers and was a part of the very same crowd the disciples were commanded to feed (Mark 6:35–44). The disciples had no food. None! And the little boy was not a disciple. So Jesus commanded his disciples to bring to him what the community had to offer. We know the end of the story – they were all fed and satisfied and there was still food left, twelve basketfuls. The message of the story is clear: do not rely on what you have – rather, work with those to whom you are sent.

Sometime later Peter would be asked to go to the house of Cornelius, a Roman officer. God had been working with the man in his own way, and Peter is asked to lead him to Christ. Peter the Jew had to be convinced of this by a special vision of unclean animals that God commanded him to eat.

The justification for the act was, whatever God has made clean is clean (Acts 10:1–30).

There is no question – Jesus did not avoid working with sinners and the non-Jews. His behaviour encourages us also to do the same, because we are sent *as* he was sent by his father (John 20:21).

There is obviously a clear biblical justification for a church *mission with the people*. But there is also a clear warning. The apostle Paul warns his followers not to put their necks under a common yoke with unbelievers (2 Cor 6:14–18). In verse 14 he says, "Do not be unequally yoked together with unbelievers. For what do righteousness and iniquity have in common? Or what fellowship can light have with darkness?" Does this mean that he, Paul, prohibits any joint actions or good deeds? Surely not. The passage does not refer to any social involvement, but rather to those actions compromising righteousness, falling into iniquity or lawlessness.[23] Paul warns against compromising the integrity of faith.[24] The warning is clear: the church being in the world may not compromise its status of not being *of* the world (John 17:16). It is in all weakness a "holy people" (1 Pet 2:9–10), an alternative community, God's prophetic voice in the world, a sign of the kingdom of God.

Being both in the world with the people and at the same time not of the world, different from the people, creates tension. And this will be, according to David Bosch, the normal condition of a missional church in the world of rebellion, injustice, and disbelief.[25] The church is invited to critically judge what to be, where to be, what to do, and when.

8.4. Strongholds of Darkness – Fight against Them

Mission takes place on the territory of an enemy. Political involvement never avoids confrontation. Injustice presupposes unjust people in power and those who seldom let go easily. Israel demonstrated this for centuries, avoiding application of the most socially just law of Jubilee, and as soon as Jesus named the issues, the leading class searched for ways to get rid of him.

---

23. See in this regard the discussion of the narrative in Philip E. Hughes, *The Second Epistle to the Corinthians*, The New International Commentary on the New Testament (Grand Rapids, MI: Eerdmans, 1962), 244–248; Paul Burnett, *The Second Epistle to the Corinthians*, The New International Commentary on the New Testament (Grand Rapids, MI: Eerdmans, 1997), 344–355; Ralph P. Martin, *2 Corinthians*, Word Biblical Commentary, Vol. 40 (Waco, TX: Word Books, 1986), 190–200.

24. Hughes, *The Second Epistle to the Corinthians*, 246; Martin, *2 Corinthians*, 197.

25. Bosch, *Transforming Mission*, 390f.

Humans, of course, are subject to deceiving spirits. The apostle Paul makes clear that we humans never fight against flesh and blood. It is not humans who deceive the world; they are being deceived. The enemies we fight against are powers and structures of darkness, demonic nature. The apostle writes: "For our struggle is not against flesh and blood, but against the rulers, against the authorities, against the powers of this dark world and against the spiritual forces of evil in the heavenly realms" (Eph 6:12).

It is true that the evil finds ways to misuse human politics to establish its sinful structures. The church will raise its voice to name those powers, knowing that Jesus came to destroy all the strongholds of the enemy. It is part of its ministry in the world too, to crush down demonic forces in prayer and fasting. This brings the spiritual dimension into all the political action of the church. It can never reduce its mission to a purely social level. As God's agent of political transformation, it brings so much more to the scene. With a gift to discern spirits, it will be able to identify the forces at play and cast out the powers that are determining the negative developments in society and destroy strongholds no political agent is ever able to fight against.

Here we see the third marker of the missionary involvement of the church in society – spiritual battle for the well-being of a nation. "We have never prayed and fasted so hard, as we do today," says the pastor of the Hope Church. "There are structures that really wish we would go back into silence and just live our religion privately. I know it is Satan and his demons. They are afraid we will become the light of the city, and then the darkness will have to flee. They are afraid we would become God's *ecclesia* and then the forces of darkness will not prevail. I tell you what – we are his *ecclesia*!"

9

The Politics of the Church – A Practice Model

9.1. The Need of a Praxis Theory

Mission in the world is mission in a certain context. Practically speaking all mission theology must be contextual. Life in different societies is, in principle, different, and it is the issues of a context that determine the political action of the church in public. The church will have to analyse the context, understand the real issues people have in order to be adequate in society and to reach a particular context with the gospel. Transformation of a given social space presupposes knowledge of the conditions ruling the context. Understanding this contextual theology means working with its threefold formula as presented by the conference of the Latin American Bishops in 1979 in Pueblo, Mexico: *See – Discern/Judge – Do*. Leonardo Boff formulated the approach in more theological terms as:[1]

1. Analysis of reality in a given context.

2. Hermeneutic interpretation of this reality according to the criteria of faith.

3. Plan of action for the praxis.

All good theology of mission will follow such or a similar formula. It comes from the praxis and it leads to the practice of life. It is asking the real questions people have, and it seeks to give proper answers of faith on the basis

---

1. Leonardo Boff, *Aus dem Tal der Tränen ins gelobte Land: er Weg der Kirche mit den Unterdrückten* (Düsseldorf: Patmos, 1982), 184f.

of what God reveals to us humans in his Holy Scriptures, considering at the same time the knowledge of the generations of Christians before us. Such theory is relevant because it is born in a real-life context and it is theologically responsible and adequate because it interprets reality through the lenses of God's revelation. It is doing theology in a way that is faithful to God's word and to the need of the people. How do we formulate such a practice-centred theory in praxis?

9.2. Praxis Cycle – Towards a Contextual Theology of Political Involvement

Appropriate missio-political involvement requires an approach which results in a "theology leading to praxis."[2] At the University of South Africa we apply the so-called praxis cycle of missionary theology originally developed by Marge Kareki.[3] The cycle uses the basic structure of the "pastoral cycle"[4] and describes five steps in a theological process:[5]

1. Involvement

2. Context analysis

3. Theological reflection

4. Spirituality

5. Planning

The working steps are cyclically ordered which means the order may be switched around if needed, or you may go back and forth until the desired result is reached.

---

2. J. N. J. (Klippies) Kritzinger, "Who Do They Say I Am?" in *An African Person in Making*, Festschrift for Prof Willem Saayman (Pretoria: UNISA Press, 2001), 147ff.

3. Kritzinger, "Who Do They Say," 147; M. Karecki, "Teaching Missiology in Context: Adaptations of the Pastoral Circle," in *The Pastoral Circle Revisited: A Critical Quest for Truth and Transformation*, eds. F. Wijsen, P. Henriot, and R. Mejia (Nairobi: Paulines, 2005), 159–173.

4. J. Holland, and P. Henriot, *Social Analysis: Linking Faith & Justice* (Marknoll, NY: Orbis, 1983).

5. Kritzinger, "Who Do They Say," 149.

```
          ┌─────────────────────┐
          │     Involvement     │
          └─────────────────────┘

┌──────────────┐              ┌──────────────┐
│ Planning for │              │   Context    │
│    action    │              │   analysis   │
└──────────────┘              └──────────────┘

┌──────────────┐              ┌──────────────┐
│ Spirituality │              │ Theological  │
│              │              │  reflection  │
└──────────────┘              └──────────────┘
```

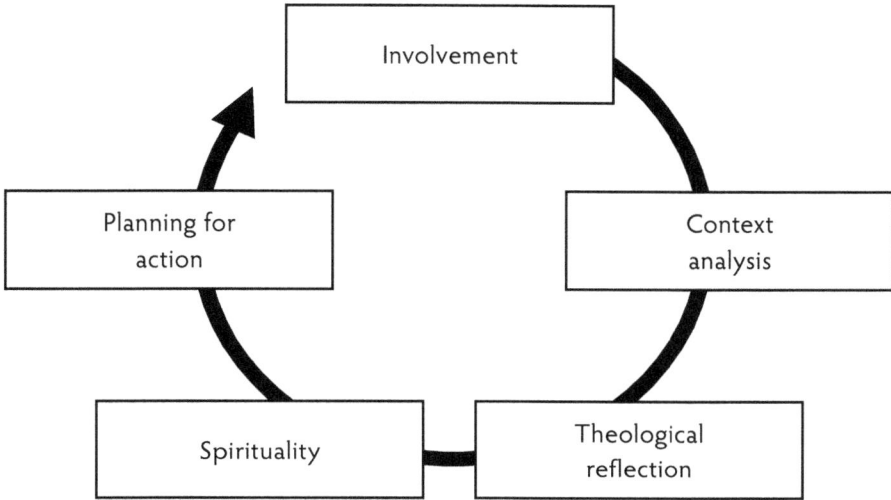

Praxis Cycle according to J. N. J. Kritzinger

The South African theologian J. N. J. Kritzinger suggests that responsible theology must include a search for ways it is to be done in the context of people for whom this theology is meant. It must enter the mission field in order to be adequate. Theological work starts, therefore, with involvement. Going to the people means to ask with Jesus the crucial question "Who do the people say I am?" (Mark 8:27–29). Only after we receive an answer we may ask – "Who do we think he is?" The answer to the first question presupposes, of course, an intensive search for an understanding of culture and life of the people we target. Without such a context analysis theological reflection is problematic, to say the least, and mission is doomed to failure. The gospel will only be understood as good news when formulated in terms of the local language and culture. Theology must reflect questions of real life and transfer the biblical revelation to the life-context of a given society in order to be relevant. Context orientation does not exclude historic reflections. To know how the church has reacted in a given situation theologically throughout its 2,000 years of history is not only helpful – it is necessary. Even more so the teaching of the Bible must be taken into consideration. But a historic discourse is not yet a theological programme for today. It offers background and clarifies perspective. Theology for the people, however, will require transfer into their context. The question, "What does tradition say about the challenges of the day?" must lead into, "What do we today say about the challenges we face?" Theology is always an art of translating the eternal truth into the context of today. It is a process of communication, which invites participation of the people in their context. Matthias Scharrer and Bernd Jochen Hilberath suggest, therefore, viewing all theology as communication.[6]

Theology is, of course, more than human reflection in context. It reflects revelation of God and as such relies on the work of God the Spirit who leads his children into all truth (John 16:13). Good theology is always pneumatic. Kritzinger requires that all Christian theologians experience the presence of the Holy Spirit as the basis for their theological work. Their spirituality will be marked by three specific attitudes:

1.   The general interest in everything they do to hear the voice of the Holy Spirit as a decisive voice.

2.   Personal experience with God transcending all areas of life. God is here not merely as an intellectual exercise, but rather a living and all-important reality.

3.   A deep sense of responsibility and respect for the people they live with and work for.

Loving God and your neighbour as yourself, the double commandment of love, transcends the cycle of contextual theology and marks its spirituality.

And finally – proper theologizing leads to praxis. The word has to become flesh in order to reveal God's glory to people (John 1:14). Contextual theology is never a theoretical concept as such, but rather a praxis theory, a *handlungstheory*, aiming towards application. It is a doing rather than thinking theology. Planning for action must, therefore, become a vital part of all theological work. Even more, planning and doing will lead to evaluation and open a new round of even deeper reflection. The cycle will turn into a spiral and theology into a *handlungstheoretical* process.

In practical terms a church going public will join the people in the community, conduct a context analysis to find the pressing issues of the day, reflect on those theologically against the biblical revelation and theological tradition in close conversation with the Spirit of God, transfer its findings into language and cultural terms of the people, and then plan action and finally act in community with the people.

---

6. Matthias Scharrer and Jochen Hilberath, *Kommunikative Theologie; Eine Grundlegung* (Mainz: Grünewald, 2002), 28f.

9.3. Acting with the People – Towards Participatory Involvement

The mission of a *church with others* is both inclusive and exclusive. Following the change pattern described to us by cultural anthropology, we will be inclusive in our involvement on the material and social levels of society and culture. We become critical and prophetic on the cognitive worldview level, and we will lovingly evangelize in spiritual and religious matters. It is understood that such comprehensive mission does not take shape overnight. It requires time, trust-building, common understanding, and an atmosphere of dialogue. Mission here is a way, a process in different stages:

1. First, you begin with service, joining in with other social players in a given community to work for the betterment of that community.

2. Second, you engage in dialogue with those you serve and those you serve with on issues relevant to the community.

3. Third, you expose yourself to questions about your faith and life and engage others in love and humility.

4. And fourth, you do not hesitate to explain the gospel as soon as you are asked for exactly this and then call people to follow Jesus if they understand and are ready to be challenged.

The four phases of mission and evangelism do not always exactly follow in a linear and chronological order. It is rather a cycle, which allows you to move back and forth towards the goal of God's mission in the world – to disciple the social reality of people. In this regard I speak about society-transformative evangelism and mission.[7] It requires presence, service, dialogue, discourse, and proclamation.

---

7. See more in Reimer, *Die Welt umarmen.*

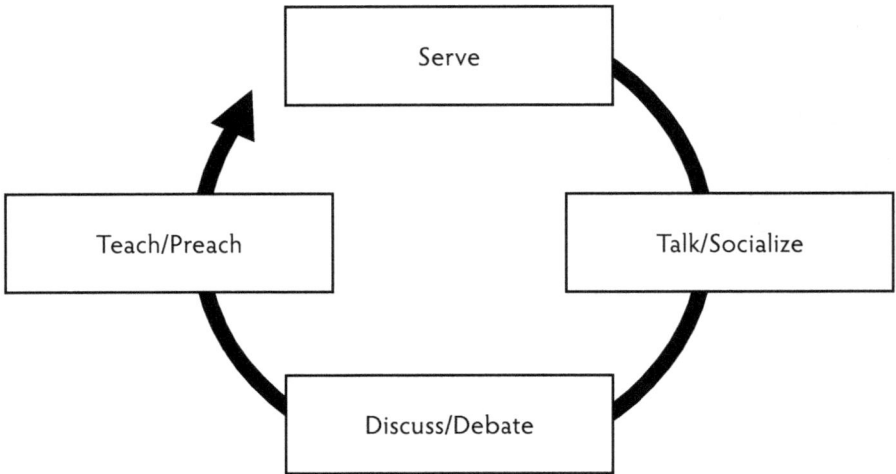

Cycle of Society-Transformative Mission

And on all levels of involvement, Christian mission will place itself "between the gospel and the world,"[8] becoming what Paul Hiebert calls "mission as mediation."[9] In fact mediation is a core competency of the church involved in God's mission to the world.[10] Serving people in joint community development projects, Christians will model to the not-yet-believers how to act as followers of Christ, feeding their imagination of what the significance of the gospel for our daily life might be. This way service becomes a thoughtful process between the person and the gospel, and then people will start asking questions, involving the servants of God in dialogue and discourse on issues they find important. Again the gospel driven answer will encourage the process further until a spiritual decision becomes a natural act.

The praxis of society-transformative mission that we are involved with proves the validity of what has been said so far. There is, for instance, the Christian Employment Agency we created years ago in a small German town called Brüchermühle to help unemployed people to earn a living. Right from the start our project operated inclusively, inviting everybody in the town to

---

8. Paul Hiebert, *The Gospel in Human Contexts: Anthropological Explorations for Contemporary Missions* (Grand Rapids, MI: Baker, 2009), 179.

9. Hiebert.

10. See for details Johannes Reimer, "Der Dienst der Versöhnung – bei der Kernkompetenz ansetzen. Zur Korrelation von Gemeinwesenmediation und multikulturellem Gemeindebau," *Theologisches Gespräch* 1 (2011): 19–35.

join hands with us. It is amazing how successful this project has become. Men and women found employment, their family life improved, and over the time many of our clients and their respective families decided to join the church and follow Jesus.[11]

Other similar projects of transformative mission have been encouraged in a number of German cities. The results are similar.[12] A comprehensive transformative approach to mission and church planting as mission-with-others, employing basic structures of joint community development, is promising.

---

11. The work has been studied by Martin Schulten. "Gesellschaftstransformativer Gemeindebau. Am Beispiel der Evangelischen Freien Gemeinde Brüchermühle und deren Sozialarbeit für Hartkernarbeitslose in der Christlichen Beschäftigungsgesellschaft." Unpublished MTh dissertation (Pretoria, SA: UNISA, 2012).

12. See some of the projects in Tobias Faix, at al., *Tat. Ort. Glaube,* Transformationsstudien, Vol. 6 (Marburg: Francke, 2014).

10

Christian Community Development (CCD)

10.1. What Is Community Development?

Community Development (CD) is the way to change and shape a society and culture. The UN defines CD as a "complex of initiatives and methodical steps to overcome social incompetence and powerlessness as well as oppression of people in a society."[1] According to Renate Schnee, CD is a "basic principle of all social work."[2] CD is never an individual venture of a single institution, but rather a joint act of all socially involved individuals, institutions and organizations in society. To achieve positive results CD must mediate intensive networking among all social actors in the community. There is a growing amount of literature reflecting different aspects of CD. M. G. Ross's 1955 book *Community Organizations: Theory and Principles* was the first scientific treatise on the topic.[3]

CD is interested in the well-being of people, approaching the felt need of the community, activating the members of the community and utilizing local resources.[4] In praxis, we distinguish between the categorical and territorial CD. Territorial CD concentrates on a marked socio-geographical space be it a village, town, city block or a neighbourhood. Categorical CD works with

---

1. Rainer Lingscheid and Gerhard Wegner, trans. *Aktivierende Gemeindearbeit* (Stuttgart-Berlin-Köln: Kohlhammer, 1990), 51–52.

2. Renate Schnee, "Gemeindewesenarbeit," online, http://www.telesozial.net/cms/uploads/tx_kdcaseengine(scriptum_Gemeindewesenarbeit_Renate_Schnee_102004.pdf, 17.

3. M. G. Ross, *Community Organization: Theory and Principles* (New York: Harper, 1955).

4. Schnee, "Gemeinwesenarbeit," 17.

a homogeneous group of people representing certain professions, social or economic status, and so on. Both forms of CD seek ways to improve the life condition of the people by activating them for action.

Besides the CD forms there are three different approaches in CD: integrative, aggressive, and catalytic-activating approach. Integrative CD (ICD) works towards stronger cooperation of all actors in a community, harmonizing all possible interests under a common philosophy of well-being. Usually the majority of people force their ideas on the whole community by using an integrative methodology in CD. To illustrate such an initiative I use the example of my own daughter Stefanie, then nine years old. The neighbourhood we were living in then did not have any playground for children. Close to our property the town was holding on to an empty piece of ground. All attempts to motivate the administration to turn the ground into a playground for children failed. My daughter activated all the children in the neighbourhood to take part in a demonstration in front of the major's office. Soon swarms of children joined the demonstration. Media representatives appeared and a real conversation started. Only months later the new playground was dedicated.

An aggressive CD (ACD) is usually used as an instrument of political intervention. Political parties with ideologically active initiatives use the instrument to influence the population.

And finally, the catalytic-activating CD (CACD) offers and initiates help for self-help. Here the neighbourhood is invited to join hands in an initiative to improve the living conditions in the area. Help is offered as self-help.

Community development is a growing market all over the world, even in developed countries of the West. Our socities have become "risk-societies" as the sociologist Ulrich Beck already prophecied in the 1980s.[5] The social space is eroding and official institutions are no longer able to provide meaningful-life conditions. Chances and challenges for CD develop as a result. All CD initiatives will search for ways to involve the creative powers of a given social space such as the political administration, the economy, the media and the local NPOs. In fact, CD always aims to influence or even shape and change such power factors in society in order that the living conditions may be changed.

---

5. Carl C. Beck, ed., *Church Planting Patterns in Japan,* 27th Hayama Men's Missionary Seminar (Tokyo: Amagi Senso, 1986).

10.2. Christian Community Development – History and Development

The church of Christ has always been socially and diaconically active. The conscious use of CD in Western churches goes back to the 1950s.[6] The American Lyle Schaller reports a growing interest in CD projects in the USA in the 1970s.[7] Schaller names a number of grounds for the growing interest.[8] He seems especially interested in the promotion and development of the individual resources of members for the well-being of a given community.[9] For him CD is an excellent tool to activate church members for community engagement.

Social transformation is the main interest of church based CD.[10] In Germany the tradition of CD related projects in the church goes back to the work of Johann Hinrich Wichern (1808–1881).[11] In his book on public involvement of the church published in 1849 he writes, "The inner mission is not a life expression outside or beside the church nor does she want to become the church . . . rather does she reveal a side of the church herself which shares life of the Spirit in faithful love to the lost, forsaken, and neglected masses."[12]

In Europe in general and Germany in particular Christian community development (CCD) was thriving strongly after World War II. Most of Europe was destroyed by the war, and millions of people lost their homes due to war and resettlements after the war. Social assistance was needed everywhere. A wave of social engagement swept over Europe. Restoration of communities became a major task for the church. But already in the 1970s, CD as one of the most effective tools of missionary involvement in society was more or less forgotten.

Reiner Lingscheid, who has studied the development of CCD in Germany in detail, concludes that the reasons why CD was pushed aside by most of the churches lay in an inadequate theological reflection of the concept on the one hand and the general disability of the church to accept its societal

---

6. Lyle E. Schaller, *Kirche und Gemeinwesenarbeit: zwischen Konflikt und Versöhnung* (Gelnhausen, Berlin: Burkhardthaus-Verlag, 1972), 3.

7. Schaller, 4ff.

8. Schaller.

9. Schaller, 8.

10. See discussion in Lingscheid, *Aktivierende Gemeindewesenarbeit*, 48ff.

11. More about the person and his social theology see in Stephan Sturm, "Funktion und Leistung: Systemtheoretischen Analysen zur Sozialtheologie von Johann Hinrich Wichern," online, http://mitglied.lycos.de/stephan_sturm/marburg2htm (Last access: 23 August 2017).

12. Wichern in Karsten Diettmann, "Diakonie zwischen Kirche und Gesellschaft," online, http://www.holmespeare.de (Last access: 23 August 2016).

responsibility on the other. The church justified its community involvement rather pragmatically and eclectically, falling way short of including CD into the genuine mission of the church in the world.[13]

10.3. In Community for the Community

CCD is theologically founded on the *missio politica* of the church. The church is by its very nature a vital agent of communal life. It is the ecclesial heart of community, salt of the earth and light of the world (Matt 5:13–16). It is a local agent, a local *ecclesia*, a gathering of chosen people called out of the community to accept responsibility for the community. Its mission territory is first and foremost the local social space. As such it will strive to become light seen by the whole city, serve all people, and become a blessing to every person in the community. Its missionary praxis will, therefore, always involve active community participation.

This makes CD a vital concept of the church's mission and church life. In fact CCD might be considered the model for active mission of the church in the world. This is clearly the case for its political mission. And as with all mission of the church, it must be seen in its reciprocal interiority. We may understand that other mission accents, such as evangelism and discipleship, are directly related to one another and with it to the community.

10.4. The Cycle of Christian Community Development

Community development follows a certain plan of action. Annette Peters names four crucial initial steps in CCD that a church interested in using CD as their format of mission will have to consider:[14]

1. Engagement in community presupposes knowledge of life in community. The church will conduct a social analysis accentuating common felt needs in community.

2. Engagement in community is only possible where resources and agents of involvement are clearly defined. The church will look for ways to activate conversation in community with the aim to

---

13. Wichern.
14. In Lingscheid, *Aktivierende Gemeindewesenarbeit*, 78.

fix the resources available and motivate active participation of all community members.

3. Engagement in community achieving lasting results will involve as many members of the community as possible. The church will seek for joint action of all actors in community to solve the problems.

4. Engagement in community requires the blessing of God. The church will spiritually back up every action in prayer and other spiritual support.

These steps in a cycle of CCD might be considered. The cycle follows the basic steps of the missionary practice cycle as discussed above. It starts with (a) involvement in the community, enters in with (b) context analysis, casts (c) vision, and develops (d) concept of change, leading to (e) planning action and (f) action, followed by (g) evaluation.

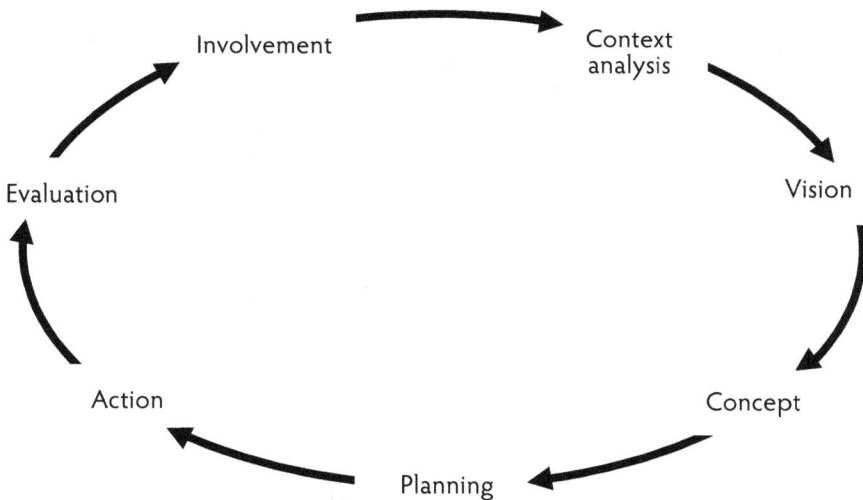

Cycle of Christian Community Development

CCD *involves* churches in community work. Basically this means that a church considering CCD has to find its community and decide to invest time and energy into this particular community of people, be it a village, a town, or a neighbourhood. Such an involvement will require a calling of God for a certain community. Knowing God is behind a task is crucial. Only when a church hears God's call for the community will it invest itself in CD permanently.

A calling is, however, not yet a *vision*. According to Bill Hybels, "Vision is a picture of the future that produces passion."[15] It is the fuel creating a movement, an energy leading to action for enlightening passion.[16] A vision is a picture of the future we have. Proper vision is never accidental. George Barna is right when he says, "You might define vision as foresight with insight based on hindsight."[17] By this he describes a view of the future that does not neglect the conditions of the present and the experience of the past. According to Barna it is God who grants his children such a vision. "Vision for the ministry is a clear mental image of a preferable future imparted by God to his chosen servants and is based upon an accurate understanding of God, self and circumstances."[18] God knows how he wants to change life in society; he determines what his vision of the future will be. Society-relevant vision brings God's idea of the world and the need of the people in context into a picture. It is a place where our love for God meets the love for our neighbour (Matt 22:37–39).[19] In these two commandments all other commandments of God are combined, says Jesus (Matt 22:40). The vision for CCD is therefore shaped by our love for God and our neighbour. A society-relevant church wants to see the kingdom of God realized in the life of community. It presupposes knowledge of God's kingdom.

A vision is not, however, a concept or practice theory yet. A concept describes the transformational process for the context in which CD is envisioned. And this, in turn, presupposes knowledge of the context. Such knowledge is acquired *in context analysis*, a process of sampling and interpreting information about the life condition in the community. This will be achieved through:

- Consulting all publically available information about the community
- Interviews with experts in the community such as the mayor, social workers, teachers, journalists, and others
- Participant observation on various levels of communal life
- Prayer walks and listening to God

---

15. Bill Hybels, *Courageous Leadership* (Zondervan: Grand Rapids, 2002), 32.
16. Hybels.
17. George Barna, *Power of Vision* (Ventura: Regal, 2003), 24.
18. Barna.
19. Deut 6:5 and Lev 19:18.

CD concentrates on community transformation, especially in the five classic areas described to us by Jesus in Matthew 25:35–36: (1) hunger and thirst; (2) loneliness; (3) poverty; (4) health; (5) societal isolation, and therefore these areas need to be inspected as deeply as possible. Only once there is knowledge of what is going on in community – both the felt needs and what the community as a whole may offer to introduce change – may concrete *conceptualizing* start.

Those planning a project need to answer the following questions:

Who does

what and *how,*

when and by which *means,*

what outcome is expected,

how is the result evaluated

and *where* will this lead?

A well-designed project leads to a successful *praxis* and allows a proper *evaluation* of achieved goals. For any CCD project, planning, action, and evaluation must include strong participation from the community in which the church is involved.

10.5. Examples from the Praxis

CCD is used by churches in many countries as a missionary tool.[20] The following examples come from different countries, contexts, and denominations. They can seldom be copied. I mention them here to encourage your own developments and ideas. Your context may require a completely different approach. The examples offer impulses rather than models.

10.5.1. Light to the World Church

Light to the World Church (LttW) was planted in 1994 by Evangelical Baptists after an evangelistic crusade organized by the Billy Graham Association.[21] In the 1990s the church was active in evangelism and discipleship. Beginning in

---

20. See an overview in Bryant Myers, *Walking with the Poor: Principles and Practices of Transformational Development* (Maryknoll, NY: Orbis, 2011).

21. Online, http://moldovabaptisthistory.blogspot.hu/p/11-13.html (Last access: 23 August 2017).

the year 2003, the church's mission began to change its focus and methods. Mission became more contextualized, flexible, and open to accept a holistic and missional vision. In 2012, the church accepted a holistic approach in mission, and together with the Christian NGO Beginning of Life (BoL) adapted a "Church of/for tomorrow" model. There are four different clusters in the church. Each of them leads services in their own style and form. Every Sunday there are around three hundred people attending church services, divided into different clusters.[22]

The Christian NGO Beginning of Life was founded in 2000 alongside LttW church as a non-governmental organization with a goal to fulfil God's mission in areas where, for different reasons, doors were closed for the evangelical church itself.[23] Since 2012 the leadership of the church leads BoL. Today BoL runs three programs: [24]

1. *Place of Change* – a holistic program for teenagers, managed by Christian teenagers themselves. Around 120 teenagers between 11 and 15 years of age attend the program.

2. *Way to success* – the program aims to prepare high school students for independent life. It is a two-year holistic program, which teaches youth life skills, critical thinking, professional orientation, and character development from a Christian perspective. There are around two hundred fifty students between 16 and 19 years old.

3. *Metamorphosis* – the program serves people who suffer from social injustice. In this program are: (a) early learning centres for moms and kids; (b) humanitarian aid centre; (c) rehabilitation centre for victims of human trafficking and social exploitation; (d) prevention centre *Dream House* for social orphans; (e) psychological art studio.

BoL also runs a few small businesses with a goal to provide jobs for the most vulnerable women.

The growth of the LttW is remarkable. What determines its growth and acceptance in society? Leaders of the church ascribe the success to the following seven characteristics.[25]

---

22. Vladimir Ubeivolk, "Interviews with the leadership of LttW and BoL," unpublished paper (Chishinew: Archives of LttW, 2015).

23. Online, http://bol.md/index.php/who-we-are (Last access: 23 August 2017).

24. Online, http://bol.md/index.php/what-we-do (Last access: 23 August 2017).

25. Ubeivolk, "Interviews."

1. Equality of different levels of involvement into the life of the whole local community/society as well as in the life of certain individuals.

2. Consistency – when people or churches face different problems, they see only the upper part of the iceberg, but missional community takes responsibility for identifying the deeper roots of a problem and finds ways to resolve it.

3. Flexibility – ability to change programs as the situation changes. Readiness to leave the comfort zone.

4. Leadership adequacy – leaders are selected and trained accordingly with their gifts and readiness, which leads to lack of autocracy. Different leaders are responsible for different decisions in their areas.

5. Freedom in choosing forms for every project and cluster.

6. Readiness to serve people outside the church, as well as inside.

7. Ability to see children and youth as equally part of church and assist them in opening their potential.

Church of/for tomorrow, as developed in Moldova, is an example of so-called net-churches, where different clusters work together not because of strong hierarchy or well-developed structures; vision and relations unite them. R. McNeal, using an example from Mike Breen's missional community in England, underlines that "people began to prefer larger gatherings for mission even more than their small-group experiences and started to hang out more in the clusters. Identity began forming around these mid-size groups, described by Breen as a sort of extended family. The communities began reproducing."[26]

Light to the World Church is today not only a growing Christian congregation, but first and foremost an agent of social change and a model repeated by other social institutions in the city and country. The stories of people who have been passing through the programs of the church and its NGO are amazing.[27]

---

26. R. McNeal, *Missional Communities: The Rise of the Post-Congregational Church* (San Francisco: Jossey-Bass, 2011), 40.

27. See examples in http://bol.md/index.php/stories (Last access: 23 August 2017).

10.5.2. Umoja – Church Based Community Development in Africa

One of the most exciting CCD programs comes from Africai Umoja. "Umoja is a community-capacity building program aimed at equipping church officials and congregants with the knowledge and tools to implement development programs in their own communities," states the Kitega Community Center near Lugazi in rural Uganda.[28] *Umoja* means togetherness in the Swahili language of East Africa. This "exciting and transformational church and community initiative helps church leaders and their congregations work together with the local community to bring about positive change for the whole community."[29]

The churches involved in Umoja "believe that the local churches can be good development partners. The local churches have strong relationships with the community and already possess some of the infrastructures needed to carry out development activities, such as buildings and land. Most importantly, church leaders and congregants already possess the motivation and passion to care for those in need. With the proper training and support, they can be great candidates to carry out well-structured development work in their communities."[30]

And this is not just a vision. Hundreds of churches in Africa, Asia, and beyond have started to apply church based community development as a tool for their holistic missions. And the results of twenty years of experience are great. Communities change and churches grow.[31]

10.5.3. New Song Community Church

The New Song Community Church (NSCC) is a fascinating congregation in Sandtown-Winchester in the inner city of Baltimore, USA. People in Sandtown are predominantly poor, asocial, and without money and work. There are many migrants among them. Life is dangerous in Sandtown. Gangs selling drugs and people in prostitution dominate the street. This is the neighbourhood of the NSCC. The church was founded by Mark R. Gornick in 1988 with the aim to

---

28. Online, http://kitegacc.org/program/community-programs/umoja-church-led-development/ (Last access: 23 August 2017).

29. Online, http://tilz.tearfund.org/en/themes/church/umoja/ (Last access: 1 August 2016).

30. Online, http://kitegacc.org/program/community-programs/umoja-church-led-development/ (Last access: 23 August 2017).

31. See case studies and tools online at http://tilz.tearfund.org/en/themes/church/church_and_community_mobilisation/open-ended_church_and_community_mobilisation/ (Last access: 23 August 2017).

serve and transform the community.[32] Gornik's dream was to bring peace and reconciliation to the community by loving and caring for the people around them. It took them two full years until the first contacts were established. Right from the start it became clear that only practical engagement for the well-being of the community would change the scepticism of the people and eventually lead them to consider a relationship with God.

Gornik and his team invited Habitat for Humanity to come to Baltimore and build and restore housing for the poorest in Sandtown. The most prominent supporter of the project became the president of United States, Jimmy Carter. The project began in 1988, and in 1992 four thousand volunteers from all over the world came to Sandtown. In a few weeks the helpers restored dozens of houses and built a few new ones. By 1994, under the leadership of NSCC, two hundred houses were completely renewed and twenty-seven newly built.[33] Many families who received the new housing joined the church in their work. A deep relationship developed.

A whole range of community-relevant ministries followed. In 1991 the New Song Community Learning Center, a centre for children, opened its doors for the community. Soon the centre became a school for all children in the community. The centre offers a number of after-school programs for children and child raising education courses for parents. The church opened the New Song Health Center, where trained doctors and nurses offered medical assistance and treatment for no cost. And in 1994, EDEN (Economic Development Employment Network), an agency offering job opportunites started. In 1994 alone, EDEN managed to successfully assist fifty unemployed neighbours to find jobs and has found jobs for many others since then.[34]

Over time many other community-related social programs were developed and launched. And the church? The small church grew in members every year, becoming a vital actor in the community. Socio-economic and spiritual development went hand-in-hand.

10.5.4. LifeBridge – a Church Enters Community

LifeBridge Christian Church in Longmont, Colorado, USA, is another interesting example of a church moving into the public space. Over one hundred

---

32. Mark R. Gornik, *To Live in Peace: Biblical Faith and the Changing Inner City* (Grand Rapids: Eerdmans, 2002), 237.

33. Gornik.

34. Gornik, 241.

years old, the former Baptist church was known in the region for its evangelistic and missionary activity.[35] The central annual missionary event usually started in September and went on until Christmas. Hundreds of different evangelistic activities took place in the city. The Christmas event absorbed a major part of the church's budget. And the church grew to a considerable size of eleven hundred members. In 1996, the lead team of the church, analyzing the growth pattern of the church, discovered that the growth of the church was largely due to transfer of believers from other churches. The church was passing out thousands of New Testaments, tracts, and other evangelistic literature to the citizens of Longmont, and offering dozens of evangelistic meetings. And the result – devastating. Only very few first-time conversations were noticed. At the same time there were still many people in the city who did not attend any Christian church and some openly rejected Jesus. What had this overly active mission-minded church done wrong? The lead team prayed, fasted, and discussed the issue, and in doing so, they discovered a major problem. The church loved God, but did not care for their neighbour. They heavily engaged in evangelism but were absent in community issues. The focus was on internal church development rather than external witness.[36] So the lead team changed direction. Rick Rusaw, the senior pastor of the church, points to the changes made:

1. They focused the church externally towards the community.

2. They avoided establishing institutions which already existed in their community, joining instead what was available, changing them from within.

3. They started to cooperate with others.

4. They decided to love and serve the community around them.

5. They invited all members of the churches and other men and women of good will to participate in their programs of community transformation.

6. They established partnerships with social institutions in their community wherever this served the cause of transformation.[37]

---

35. Rick Rusaw and Eric Swanson, *The Externally Focused Church* (Loveland, CO: Group, 2004), 37f.

36. Rusaw, 49.

37. Rusaw.

And a new era began for the church. Typical of the change is the former Christmas action. Instead of doing classic evangelism, the leadership of the church introduced "A Time to Serve," a program of different community-related services run from September to Christmas. Many opportunities to serve people, ranging from cleaning up parks and recreation areas to painting the walls in a public school or helping small businessmen to restructure their businesses, were listed. Church members could select where and what they would be interested in doing. The program was also introduced to the wider community. Many signed up.[38] Among those who joined, more than fifteen hundred people joined the program the first time the programme was offered. Six thousand hours of service were delivered in the end.[39] And the reaction of the people in the city was more than overwhelming. This experience lead to the renaming of the church and restructuring the church's ministry. The externally focused LifeBridge Church was born, and community development became the actual format of its mission. Today the church is involved in numerous ministries in Longmont. Serving the people, the church has slowly regained the trust of its neigbours. Many of them decided to join the ministries and later on the church, giving their lives to Christ.[40] Today more than 4,000 people attend the extended church. To be the heart of the community and not the outpost of society – this is what the church seeks to be, says one of the pastors.[41] And God blesses LifeBridge in every regard.

---

38. Rusaw, 40f.
39. Rusaw, 43.
40. Rusaw, 43–45.
41. Rusaw, 44.

11

Community Centred Church – a Question of Leadership?

11.1. Community-Minded Leadership

A community-relevant church will require community-minded leadership. Traditional church leadership will hardly develop a church involved in public discourse.[1] What is needed is leadership that is both theologically founded in Scripture and deeply committed to God's mission in the world. Such leadership will be contextual in form and missional in spirit. Kenneth L. Gallahan in his book on effective church leadership offers a helpful chart correlating the above mentioned crucial categories.[2]

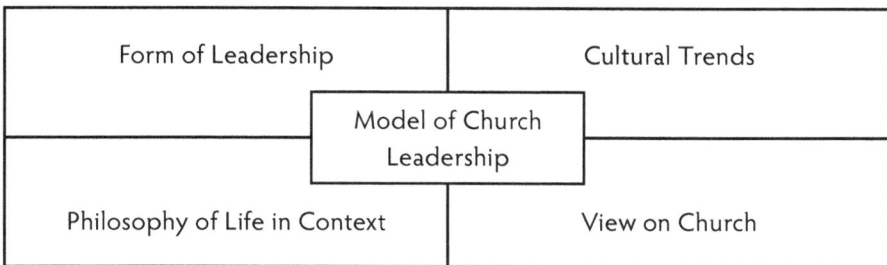

Form of Leadership		Cultural Trends
	Model of Church Leadership	
Philosophy of Life in Context		View on Church

Categories Determining Church Leadership

---

1. Callahan compares different traditional and internally focused models of leadership and concludes that most of them will by definition fail to serve mission. See Kennon Callahan, *Effective Church Leadership: Building on the Twelve Keys* (San Francisco, CA: Harper & Row, 1990), 3f.

2. Callahan, 37f.

Following the categories of Gallahan, we search for an adequate model of leadership in a church with a political mission.

11.2. Theologically Adequate Eldership

In his book *Mission on the Way* the American missiologist, Charles Van Engen, points to the fact that effective mission of the church requires mission-minded leadership.[3] Van Engen quotes Ephesians 4:11–12 to prove his case. Here we read, "So Christ himself gave the apostles, the prophets, the evangelists, the pastors and teachers, to equip his people for works of service, so that the body of Christ may be built up."

It is obvious that Paul, who writes the letter to the Ephesians, envisions a team of gifted people leading the church to growth. In his estimation, to expect a single pastor to conform to the content of the text is literally an illusion. George Barna goes as far as to say that a one-person-leadership will by definition not be able to facilitate each member of the church to the ministry assigned to him or her by God.[4] The genius of the New Testament model is called APEPT – a team of five: apostle, prophet, evangelist, pastor, and teacher. They are set out by God to facilitate the work of ministry.[5] Let's examine what this means for praxis.

11.3. Strategic Competence

The *apostle* is named first in our list. It is not difficult to find out what ministry apostles were involved in. Paul himself and the twelve disciples of Jesus were called apostles and beside them a whole number of other men and even one women: Matthias (Acts 1:26), James (Gal 1:19), Barnabas (Acts 14:3, 12, 14), Apollos (1 Cor 4:6–9), Timotheus (Acts 19:22), Silas/Silvanus (Acts 15:22), Tychicus (2 Tim 4:12), Judas (Acts 15:22), Andronicus (Rom 16:7) and even

---

3. Charles Van Engen, *Mission on the Way: Issues in Mission Theology* (Grand Rapids: Baker Academic,1996), 233.

4. George Barna, *The Power of Team Leadership* (Colorado Springs: WaterBrook Press, 2001), 18ff.

5. See more in Barna, *The Power of Team Leadership*.

Junia, a woman (Rom 16:7). There are altogether thirty-two names that *expresis verbis* are called apostle.[6]

There are obviously reasons why the term apostle is largely avoided today.[7] One of them is the use of the term by certain sects, for instance the New Apostolic Church. In the majority world, however, such a caution is seldom practiced. The freedom exercised in the South might encourage all Christians in the world to use the term applying its original biblical meaning.

The New Testament term, *apostolos*, stands for a missionary figure sent to proclaim the gospel of the kingdom and build the church as a living sign of the kingdom.[8] The classic example of an apostle is Paul.[9] His life and ministry is best reported in the Scriptures. The report allows for recovering an apostolic profile. Apostles like Paul planted (1 Cor 3:6) and solidified churches (Rom 1:11) teaching them to become responsible for mission. He is best described as a missionary and a missionary strategist. How does an apostle lead the church? How does he facilitate members of the church to do what God is calling them to do? The apostle Paul writes 1 Corinthians 3:5–9:

> What, after all, is Apollos? And what is Paul? Only servants, through whom you came to believe – as the Lord has assigned to each his task. I planted the seed, Apollos watered it, but God has been making it grow. So neither the one who plants nor the one who waters is anything, but only God, who makes things grow. The one who plants and the one who waters have one purpose, and they will each be rewarded according to their own labour. For we are fellow workers in God's service; you are God's field, God's building.

Paul seems to define his ministry as the planting and watering of faith. In other words people are led to faith and grow in faith through an apostle. David Cannistraci, who has studied the apostolic ministry in depth, summarizes this ministry with the same two terms: planting and growing faith.[10]

Paul calls Apollos as well as himself in 1 Corinthians 3:6–7 a *ho psyteuon*, a planter, and a *ho potizon*, a waterer. Both are crucial for spiritual growth and

---

6. David Cannistraci, *Apostles and the Emerging Apostolic Movement: A Biblical Look at Apostleship and How God Is Using It to Bless His Church Today* (Ventura: Gospel Light Publications, 2001), 67. Cannistraci (100ff) discusses the person and role of Junia at length.

7. See for instance Wayne Grudem, *Systematic Theology*, 911.

8. *TWNT*, I, 421f.

9. *TWNT*, I, 438.

10. Cannistraci, *Apostles*, 111.

find a rich tradition in the Old as well as New Testament writings.[11] Both imply teaching.[12] It is impressive to see how the apostle Paul exercised the apostolic task by planting numerous churches and leading them to maturity, for example, in Antioch (Acts 11:26), Corinth (Acts 18:1–11), Ephesus (Acts 19:9; 20:31) and elsewhere. As soon as he saw the church stable enough he appointed local leadership and moved on to evangelize and plant new churches in areas yet to be reached with the gospel (see for instance Rom 1:1–14).

He is in principle interested in promoting God's kingdom in the world and he does so strategically. He understands the context and finds ways to contextualize the gospel by becoming a Jew to the Jews and a Greek to the Greeks (1 Cor 9:19–23). The mission of the church is basically apostolic in strategy. It requires apostolic leadership to define and guide the church in its wholistic mission including its political mission

11.4. Spiritual Competence

Second, Paul mentions *prophets*. They are equally called to facilitate the Holy Spirit for the work of their ministry. Prophets are crucial for the mission of the church.[13]

According to the Old Testament a prophet is a person who receives a divine message,[14] which needs to be publicly announced.[15] The word of a prophet allows a theological interpretation of social and political events. It is the prophetic voice that interprets the fall of Samaria in 721 BC in the light of Israel's relationship to God.[16]

---

11. Planting as a theological category is mentioned for example in Gen 15:17; 2 Sam 7:10; Pss 1:3; 80:16; 92:14; Jer 2:21; 11:17; 42:10; Matt 15:13; 21:33; Rom 6:5; Jas 1:21; etc. And for watering see Isa 44:3 and others.

12. For example Heinz-Dietrich Wendland, *Die Briefe an die Korinther,* NTD Vol. 3 (Göttingen: Vandehoeck & Ruprecht, 1976), 33.

13. See R. Schnackenburg, *Der Brief an die Epheser,* EKK, Vol. 10 (Zürich/Einsiedeln/Köln: Benzinger/Neukirchener, 1982), 183; Markus Barth, *Ephesians 4–6: A New Translation with Introduction and Commentary,* The Anchor Bible. Vol. 32a (New York, London, Toronto, Sydney, Auckland: Doubleday, 1960), 435–436; etc.

14. hebr. *nabi* = one who has been called; *roaeh* = one who sees; and *isch ha aelohim* = a man of God. See more in O. Betz, "Prophetie," in *Das große Bibellexikon,* Vol. 3, trans. H. Burkhardt, F. Grünzweig, F. Laubach, and G. Meier, 1231–1240 (Wuppertal und Gießen: Brockhaus, 1990).

15. Grudem, *Systematic Theology*, 13ff.

16. About prophecy as a revealed interpretation of history, F. Flückinger, "Das Wesen biblischer Prophetie," in *Zukunftserwartung in biblischer Sicht,* trans. Gerhard Meier. Wuppertal: Brockhaus, 1983), 22ff.

The prophet reveals a different, a divine perspective to the historic event. He determines where God is in human experience. His word announces God's judgment and salvation in a concrete, historic context. Max Turner says that prophecy is God's way to express his divine will in a concrete situation with his people.[17] Prophecy in the New Testament follows a similar pattern.[18] Here too God reveals his will in a life situation of the people. We see how missionary personnel are called to mission (Acts 13:1–3), personal guidance in ministry is given (Acts 16:6–13; 18:10), warning of approaching famine is issued (Acts 11:28) and personal destiny predicted (Acts 20:23; 21:4, 11). In all of this God speaks directly and concretely. Croucher concludes that all prophecy is God's direct communication in a certain context. Paul warns the church in Thessalonica: "Do not quench the Spirit. Do not treat prophecies with contempt" (1 Thess 5:19–20).

The New Testament contains many prophetic texts. Aune[19] and with him Turner[20] identified many prophetic sayings, both adapted Old Testament prophecies as well as new prophetic words. Aune counts fifty-nine prophesies in the New Testament.[21] He puts them into the following six categories:

- Words of assurance (Acts18:9; 23:11; 27:23–24; 2 Cor 12:9; etc.)
- Words of guidance (Gal 5:21; Acts 13:2; 21:4; 2 Thess 3:6; etc.)
- Words promising salvation (Rev 14:13; 19:9; etc.)
- Words of judgment (Acts 13:9–11; 1 Cor 14:37–38; Gal 1:8–9)
- Words of legitimation (1 Cor 12:3) and self-promotion (Rev 1:8, 17)
- Words predicting the eschatological future (Rom 11:25–26; 1 Cor 15:51–52; 1 Thess 4:16–17)

The New Testament Scriptures prove the nature of the prophetic word as direct and concrete speaking into a given situation.[22] Prophecy actualizes God's word for the time and space. Paul expresses this in 1 Corinthians 14:3 saying, "But everyone who prophesies speaks to men for their strengthening, encouraging and comfort."

---

17. Max Turner, *The Holy Spirit and Spiritual Gifts Then and Now* (Grand Rapids: Baker Academics, 1996), 190.

18. See more in Turner, *The Holy Spirit*, 187ff; Aune, *Prophecy in Early Christianity and the Ancient Mediterranean World* (Grand Rapids: Eerdmans, 1983).

19. Aune, *Prophecy*, 247f, 317f.

20. Turner, *The Holy Spirit*, 204–205.

21. Aune, *Prophecy*, 441; Turner, *The Holy Spirit*, 205.

22. Aune, *Prophecy*, 338.

Strengthening, in Greek, *oikodome*, means to mentor a person in his or her proper position. Here it means to help a Christian find the right place and ministry in following Christ. The prophetic word orients Christians in their walk with God. A good example of this is the life and ministry of the apostle Paul. He begins his mission through the ministry of prophets (Acts 13:1–12) and the prophetic word accompanies his missionary endeavours – compare for instance Acts 20:23.

Encouraging, in Greek, *paraklesis,* reveals the right way of following Jesus and points to the possible pitfalls.[23] The paracletic prophetic word analyses the scheme of life and ministry, points to everything ungodly and corrects the path of a believer or the church as a whole.

And finally comfort, in Greek, *paramythia,* describes God's gracious support on the way to God's future (1 Cor 14:29–33). Together the three terms describe God's personal involvement in shaping the church's life and ministry in concrete time and space.

According to 1 Corinthians 14:29–32, prophets minister in the church and especially in worship services. Men and women were involved (1 Cor 11:5). Paul even expects the whole congregation to prophecy in an orderly manner, one prophet following the other.

In 1 Corinthians 14:29 we read: "Two or three prophets should speak, and the others should weigh carefully what is said." It becomes clear prophecy must be proved to be correct. And it is the church as a discerning community who judges over what is being said. Other examples show that prophets were also exercising their gift outside of worship meetings. Agabus, for instance, warned Paul of his imprisonment in Jerusalem (Acts 21:10–11). Or the daughters of Philip the Evangelist seemed to exercise their gift at home (Acts 21:9). The New Testament church knew and cherished the prophetic word. Peter encouraged the church to hold on to the prophetic word (2 Pet 1:19), even in times where many false prophets visited the churches and created unrest (2 Pet 2:1–22). There seems to be no possible alternative to prophecy. They constitute the core of the apostolic leadership of the church (Eph 4:11). This is especially true when it comes to mission. It is the Spirit of God who "when he comes, he will prove the world to be in the wrong about sin and righteousness and judgment" (John 16:8). And he speaks through his prophets.

---

23. See 1 Cor 14:24–25 using the term for the worship gathering of the church.

11.5. Communication Competence

The third competence the apostle Paul mentions in Ephesians 4:11 is *evangelists*. The word derives from the Greek *euangelion* and means good news. To communicate the good news then describes what an evangelist does. The concept is presented in the New Testament in more than fifty instances; however only three times is the evangelist mentioned. Besides in our core text, in Ephesians 4:11, Philip, a deacon of the Church in Jerusalem (Acts 21:8) and Timothy (2 Tim 4:5) are called evangelists. What does an evangelist do? Walter Klaiber argues that the term derives its meaning from the Old Testament idea of a messenger of joy who announces salvation of the Lord and peace to Israel.[24] The messenger of peace is frequently used in the Old Testament.[25] Indeed the Greek word for a messenger *angellos* and *euangelizesthai* correlate. An evangelist, *euangelos,* is, as it seems, a messenger announcing the victory of God over the forces of darkness. David J. Bosch points to Jesus who proclaimed the good news of the kingdom (Mark 1:15).[26] His evangelization was proclamation of the reign of God in word and deed.[27]

The examples of Philip and Timothy demonstrate what the ministry of an evangelist in the apostolic church contained:[28] Philip proclaimed "the kingdom of God and the name of Jesus the Christ" (Acts 8:12) as did Timothy, a "co-worker in God's service in spreading the gospel of Christ" (1 Thess 3:2). The evangelists were, it seems, men and women involved in active proclamation and training of church members for proclamation of the gospel in word and deed. They were gifted to find the "hearing of the people."[29] They knew how to communicate the gospel effectively. Without them the church is in danger of missing people in the presentation of the gospel. All mission is political and

---

24. Walter Klaiber, *Ruf und Antwort, Biblische Grundlagen einer Theologie der Evangelisation* (Gütersloh: Gütersloher Verlagshaus, 1990), 34.

25. Isa 61:1 Nahum 1:15 and Isa 52:7. See also Rom 10:15.

26. David J. Bosch in Karl Müller and Theo Sundermeier, eds., *Dictionary of Mission: Theology, History, Perspectives* (Eugene, OR: Wipf & Stock, 2006), 151.

27. Bosch defines evangelism as "(a) the activities involved in spreading the gospel, or (b) theological reflections on these activities." And evangelization is defined as "(a) the process of spreading the gospel, or (b) the extent to which it has been spread" (Bosch, *Transforming Mission*, 409).

28. According to I. Howard Marshall, "Who Were the Evangelists?" in *The Mission of the Early Church to the Jews and Gentiles,* ed. by Jostein Adna and Hans Kvalbei (Tübingen: Mohr-Siebeck, 2000), 251ff, evangelists in the apostolic age were responsible for the creating and ordering of all proclamation of a local church.

29. Marshall, 179.

communicative at the same time. The gift of an evangelist is crucial in order to add effectiveness to mission.

11.6. Mentoring Competence

Christian mission requires the spiritual, emotional, and personal stability of those involved in mission. According to Ephesians 4:11 it is the task of a *pastor* to lead the members of the church to stability.[30] He is the counsellor of the church and leads the congregation to maturity, to a state where the members become able to support and counsel each other (Col 3:16).[31] "The church is," as Dietrich Bonhoeffer says, "a place of love and acting in favour of each other."[32]

The responsibility of the pastor is not limited, however, to the internal counselling in the church. Paul includes all people in this ministry. In Colossians 1:27–28 we read: "To them God has chosen to make known among the Gentiles the glorious riches of this mystery, which is Christ in you, the hope of glory. We proclaim him, admonishing and teaching everyone with all wisdom, so that we may present everyone perfect in Christ." Paul mentions here two key terms: *kataggello*, a Greek term meaning public proclamation[33] and *noutetein,* meaning changing the way one thinks in practical issues of life. Pastoral ministry concentrates on edification and education of people in accordance with the gospel. Pastors are mission mentors.

The church of Christ is God's place in which people find their personal and spiritual maturity and identity. It is a genuine obligation for pastors gifted with *parakalesis*, an ability to comfort and admonish, to strengthen and facilitate the believers (Rom 12:8). They are given "counselling competence"[34] which according to Ziemer consists of the following categories: personal, communicative hermeneutic, spiritual, and conceptual.[35] In other words, if pastors want to stay missional, they must have:

---

30. The Christian church has from the earliest times of its history promoted such a view. See the discussion in Jürgen Ziemer, *Seelsorgelehre, Eine Einführung für Studium und Praxis* (Göttingen: Vandenhoeck & Ruprecht, 2000), 62ff.

31. See Ziemer, *Seelsorgelehre,* 121f. The church is the primary agent of counselling (Ziemer, *Seelsorgelehre,* 123).

32. Ziemer, *Seelsorgelehre,* 122.

33. See for instance Joachim Gnilka, *Theologie des Neuen Testaments,* Herders theologischer Kommentar zum Neuen Testament, Supplementband (Freiburg-Basel-Wien: Herder, 1991), 103.

34. Ziemer, *Seelsorgelehre,* 182.

35. Ziemer, 182–185.

A mature personality

An ability to be an effective communicator

A knowledge of human nature and ability to analyze human behaviour

A deep personal spirituality

A biblical and theological understanding

One might add sensitivity, or as H. Tacke puts it, "a fine hearing to sense the cry of the needy for help."[36]

Pastors enable and supervise a transforming process of change in individual lives and consequently in a whole community. Where their ministry is missing, social indifference will dominate the church and the community. As a result the church soon turns into an immature sect with an inferiority complex, which will never be able to change and transform the society it is in. Pastoral competence is never an option – it is a necessity for the church involved in public ministry.

11.7. Theological Competence

A missional church will be a church based in Scripture. It follows Jesus as its model. He began his ministry incarnating God's word into human reality (John 1:1–14). In its midst, God's word of reconciliation will take shape and become the reality by which people live (2 Cor 5:18). In order to do so it has to know and understand the word of God. This is the task of *teachers* in an apostolic team.

The importance of teaching is underlined by the Great Commission in Matthew 28:19–20. Jesus commands his disciples: "Therefore go and make disciples of all nations, baptizing them in the name of the Father and of the Son and of the Holy Spirit, and teaching them to obey everything I have commanded you. And surely I am with you always, to the very end of the age." Disciples are made by teaching! And consequently the first church accentuated teaching as one of their most important ministries right after it was founded on the day of Pentecost (see Acts 2:42–47). Paul requires teaching qualities from the church leaders (1 Tim 3:1–7). The teacher in an apostolic team is important.

---

36. H. Tacke, *Glaubenshilfe als Lebenshilfe* (Neukirchen-Vluyn: Neukirchener Verlag, 1975), 92ff.

Such teachers are, however, more than trained and knowledgeable specialists in Christian doctrine. They are, according to the American theologian Gangel, first and foremost spirit gifted and guided.[37] God gives them the gift of teaching (Rom 12:6–7; Eph 4:11; 2 Tim 2:2). He is like his master was, "a teacher from God" (John 3:2). And how does Jesus teach? The following might summarize his teaching ministry:

1. Jesus often refers to the Scriptures of the Old Testament. His teaching is bound to the revelation of God in Scripture.

2. Jesus's teaching is marked by authority. In Matthew 7:28–29 we read how his listeners were astonished about how and what he preached, "for he was teaching them as one who had authority, and not as their teachers of the law." His authority was obviously due to the fact that words and deeds in Jesus's teaching correlated. Wherever he spoke, signs and wonders followed.

3. Jesus's teaching came out of a close relationship with God, his Father. He himself states, "I do nothing on my own, but speak just what the Father taught me" (John 8:28). His teaching comes from *above*, inspired by God. He is a teacher *from God* and not just a teacher about God.

4. Jesus teaches contextually. He uses the situation in which he finds his listeners. Nicodemus came to him during the night (John 3:1–21). He teaches in the synagogue on the Sabbath (e.g. Matt 4:23; 9:35), engages critics and enemies in disputes (e.g. Mark 12:13; 9:10–14), and in constant personal teaching of his disciples (Matt 5, 6, 7).

5. Jesus takes time. Teaching requires time. Jesus facilitates a process. An example of this is the story with Lazarus. Martha and Mary let him know that Lazarus is critically ill. But Jesus was in no hurry. He came late. His friend had died. And then the story starts to unfold. Jesus raises Lazarus from the dead and teaches his disciples a basic lesson – he is the resurrection and life (John 11:25). It is fascinating to see how the Master patiently keeps teaching his disciples, even when they should have known better long before.

Teachers follow Jesus the master teacher. They lay foundations for an adequate mission.

---

37. Tacke, 37f.

11.8. Less Is Fatal

Missional church development targeting society transformation is a complicated matter. It needs effective leadership. God has installed in the church his APEPT: a team able to sort out issues of the day by asking strategic, analytical, comunicative questions and at the same time care for the personal and theological development of all church members. It is important to notice that it is God himself who ordained the team, and he decides what is crucially important.

The success of the society-transformative mission of the church depends on the involvement of all members of the church. They need to be prepared to do the particular ministry God has called them to do (Eph 4:12). This is the way for both to grow – the individual beliver and the church (Eph 4:13–16).

Here lies one of the major problems in the modern church. Ogden talks about the "unfinished business" of the Reformation in Europe. The reformers were rightly underlining the priesthood of all believers but failed to name ways to accomplish the task. Unleashing church members for ministry may amount to "new reformation;"[38] it is the task of APEPT. Many churches in the world seem to have discovered this basic truth.[39] Leadership structures requiring less will never accomplish the task. The church, in a globalized and postmodern world, seeks to proclaim the good news of God's kingdom in conditions that are often complicated and challenging. Strategic and prophetic insights will be crucial, and communication in a multicultural and multi-optional world will require expertise that only God is able to give. To rely on past experience as some of the evangelical churches do is dangerous, and the backdoors are closed; the options are few. It is as L. Sweet says, "You sink or swim."[40] A well guided and politically active missional church will swim, as Jesus promised.

---

38. Greg Ogden, *Unfinished Business: Returning the Ministry to the People of God* (Grand Rapids: Zondervan, 1990), 189f.

39. See among others Kenneth O. Gangel, ed., *Team Leadership in Christian Ministry* (Chicago: Moody Press, 1997); George Gladis, *Leading the Team-Based Church* (San Francisco: Jossey-Bass, 1999).

40. Leonard I. Sweet, *Soul Tsunami: Sink or Swim in the New Millenium Culture* (Grand Rapids: Zondervan, 1999).

12

At Home as Well as Abroad

12.1. Local Roots and Global Wings

The local character of *ecclesia* does not limit the mission of the church to a given community. The opposite is true. Becoming an obedient community of the kingdom of God with a distinct local expression, incarnating into the context and serving its neighbours by transforming the community to a better place of living, the church will experience the leadership of the Holy Spirit as the major factor in its mission. He is the Lord of mission (2 Cor 3:17). And he leads the church into all truth (John 16:13). Where he takes initiative, the disciples of Christ will soon become witnesses unto the end of the world (Acts 1:8).

Local mission always opens the door for world mission. And local socio-political engagement leads to global responsibility. Christian mission is glocal by its nature. The church has a global commission and a local expression. Some may say it has deep local roots and powerful global wings, as a result of it belonging to the Lord of Lords, the creator and the sustainer of the world.

Global involvement of the church is theologically motivated. The modern world, however, establishes still another argument – the world around us is increasingly becoming global. Decisions made elsewhere in the world will soon influence developments locally. The economy is to a great extent controlled by multinational corporations. They seem less interested in developing local communities and more interested in using them to raise profit for themselves. As a result communities rise and fall economically in direct dependency on global economic developments. Scores of uprooted global nomads follow the flow of capital investments, both enriching and depriving local communities. It is literally impossible to stay inside local parameters by developing and transforming life locally. A missional and politically responsible church will have to engage in global mission, not only theologically, but also pragmatically.

What does this mean in practical terms? Where is the church invited to accept global political responsibility? How does this become practical? Kingdom mission is all about practice. What are ways and tools to express God's heart in a world of need and injustice?

12.2. Globalization – Structures and Powers of Injustice

12.2.1. Economic Injustice

In a globalized capitalist world multinational corporations are the new rulers of the day. They buy huge properties in countries with natural resources, exploit them, and leave burned ground behind them. They buy the best and the most fruitful land, destroy the native agricultural production, and establish industrial companies growing coffee instead of bread, gum instead of fruit. Their philosophy is to achieve maximum profit. The destiny of the people in the place is of little to no importance to them. It is often computers who decide where and in what the companies invest. Most of them are capital and profit driven. Communities serve as a means to make more money. They serve the mammon and confront, therefore, the culture and attitude of the church. Jesus clearly says, "You cannot serve God and mammon at the same time." Followers of Jesus will never accept such structures, and if and when they do, they have left the ways of Jesus.

The church of Christ is a global reality. Christianity is the largest world religion. Theoretically Christians are able to effectively interfere in unjust economic structures, if only we understand our calling and mission. Just imagine a billion people in the global world boycotting those multinational corporations who foster injustice. I can't imagine that those profit-sick agencies of mammon would continue with their praxis of exploitation. The global church would change the world. But by staying out of politics it indirectly supports injustice, and by buying the products of the mammonists it actively supports injustice.

The example of my own church I was pastoring years back illustrates what is possible. Our three hundred members decided to boycott the local discounters until they removed certain products from their shelves. Not only did we not buy their coffee, or clothes made by children etc., we told them we would never even return to their stores until the list of unjustly produced products disappeared from their stores. We advertised our action in the local media. Soon hundreds of other Christians and other socially concerned citizens of our city – who did not share our faith but shared our position in regard to injustice – joined us. Months later the discounters removed the unjustly produced products from the shelves. Indeed, they tried to bring in new and less recognizable products, and we had to monitor them. The success of our action impressed me deeply. We Christians can impact the world, if we will only do it!

12.2.2. The Global Refugee Problem

Profit maximization, as the basic philosophy of operation of the globalized economy is responsible for a growing injustice and wealth distribution in the world. While the West grows wealthier by the day, other parts of the world, Africa for instance, lose the very basic foundation for existence. Millions of people live at the edge of survival, among them many Christians. The church will raise its voice against such developments.

Left without basic means for life many of them flee to the West. Millions of refugees worldwide are on the move to the north. Europe is seen as the secure haven, but the way there is dangerous and often life threatening. After arriving in Europe, only a few of the refugees find the means to integrate into their new world. The church of Christ is called to become a voice for all the deprived and desperate people. It will name the issues leading to the refugee crisis in the world. It will seek for practical but also political solutions and become both an advocate and a helper for those on the move to a better life.

12.2.3. Peace Mission

Refugee highways not only exist because of global economic injustice. It is the never-ending chain of wars forcing millions of people to leave their countries, which are devastated by military actions. Regional wars are driven by local and international interests and power struggles, and they clearly are made possible by a mighty military industry, selling their death-bringing products everywhere in the world. It is the military-industrial complex which appears as a main factor in the world's warfare. The prophetic voice of the church must be raised, pointing to those who make their profit out of the killing of millions of innocent people. The church can't keep quiet and stay out of the war rhetoric of their national governments. It must name those who start wars in the name of their own economic and political ambitions, even if this would mean persecution.

"If we take a clear position on the conflict going on in Ukraine," says a friend of mine in Russia, "then the government will come down on us. So we better pull out of all politics and let the government do whatever they believe is best for our country. Our responsibility is evangelism."

"And while you say nothing, your government is involved in killing innocent people, some of them your brothers and sisters in Christ. Can you accept this?" I replied.

"Our mission is spiritual," continued my friend and marked the problem of an apolitical church.

No, the church will not stay out of the conflict. It can't accept killings in the name of politics. It will name the issues, it will interfere, and it will engage in peace mediation, because it is an ambassador of reconciliation (2 Cor 5:18). Its message is a message of peace; its Lord is the prince of peace. It promotes life and not death.

12.2.4. Fighting the Criminal Structures

The refugee highways are plastered with criminal structures. Many of the deprived become victims of human trafficking, exploited in many ways. Just think of sexual exploitation. Millions of young women and men, often children, are sold into sexual slavery. Globalization is opening doors to a new age of slavery with its horrible culture of misuse, rape, and exploitation. The church of Christ cannot keep quiet about all of this. It will raise its voice in public, name the issues, and find ways to release the slaves from their bondage.

An impressive example of engagement against the criminal structures and for freedom of all those enslaved is the Church of Peace in Chishinew, Moldova. Twenty years ago the small Baptist church started to identify Moldavian sex slaves in Western Europe and organized a way for them to flee their misery and bondage. The programme grew to an amazing size. Soon advocacy programs for those in bondage came into the picture. Today the church is an amazing example of a politically active and spiritually growing church in one of the poorest countries of Europe.

12.3. Seeing and Praying

Missio politica starts with open eyes. Jesus urges his disciples to see the fields ready for harvest and pray to God, the Father, for a solution (Matt 9:38) and then he sends them to the lost sheep of the house of Israel with a message of restoration and peace. All kingdom mission starts with *seeing* and *praying*. The church needs to be introduced to this basic step of missionary involvement.[1] And a church with wide-open eyes will see the local and global powers of destruction and engage in active action to stop destruction and introduce life. The areas of global involvement might be expanded. The world is highly dynamic. New issues are coming up daily. A politically aware church will discover them and engage wherever the Lord of mission calls it to. Obedient to the Lord, it will soon make a difference in a world in need of change and transformation.

---

1. A great tool is the booklet published by Steve Bradbury and Allan Harkness, *Seeing and Praying: The Meaning and Motivation of Christian Discipleship* (Lidcombe, Australia: Scripture Union, 2000).

Bibliography

Aune, David. *Prophecy in Early Christianity and the Ancient Mediterranean World.* Grand Rapids: Eerdmans, 1983.

Barna, George. *Power of Vision.* Ventura: Regal, 2003.

———. *The Power of Team Leadership.* Colorado Springs: WaterBrook Press, 2001.

Barnett, Paul. *The Second Epistle to the Corinthians.* The New International Commentary on the New Testament. Grand Rapids, MI: Eerdmans, 1997.

Barth, Karl. *Church Dogmatics IV/3.* Edinburgh: T&T Clark, 1962.

Barth, Markus. *Ephesians 4–6: A New Translation with Introduction and Commentary.* The Anchor Bible. Volume 32a. New York, London, Toronto, Sydney, Auckland: Doubleday, 1960.

Beck, Carl C., ed. *Church Planting Patterns in Japan.* Twenty-Seventh Hayama Men's Missionary Seminar. Tokyo: Alvasi Senso, 1986.

Betz, O. "Prophetie." In *Das große Bibellexikon.* Vol. 3. Translated by H. Burkhardt, F. Grünzweig, F. Laubach, and G. Meier, 1231–1240. Wuppertal & Gießen: Brockhaus, 1990.

Beyerhaus, Peter. "Zur Theologie der Religionen im Protestantismus." In *Kerygma und Dogma* 15 (1969): 100–104.

Beyerlein, Kraig, and Mark Chaves. "The Political Activities of Religious Congregations in the United States." *Journal for the Scientific Study of Religion* 42, no. 2 (June 2003): 229–246.

Blauw, Johannes. *The Missionary Nature of the Church: A Survey of Biblical Theology of Mission.* New York, NY: McGraw-Hill, 1962.

Boff, Leonardo. *Aus dem Tal der Tränen ins gelobte Land: Er Weg der Kirche mit den Unterdrückten.* Düsseldorf: Patmos, 1982.

Bonhoeffer, Dietrich. *Letters and Papers from Prison.* Enlarged edition. London: SCM, 1971.

Bonino, Jose Miguez. *Christians and Marxists.* Grand Rapids: Eerdmans, 1976.

Bosch, David J. *Transforming Mission: Paradigm Shifts in Theology of Mission.* Maryknoll, NY: Orbis, 1991.

Bradbury, Steve, and Allan Harkness. *Seeing and Praying: The Meaning and Motivation of Christian Discipleship.* Lidcombe, Australia: Scripture Union, 2000.

Bright, J. *The Kingdom of God in Bible and Church.* London: Lutterworth, 1955.

Callahan, Kennon. *Effective Church Leadership: Building on the Twelve Keys.* San Francisco, CA: Jossey-Bass, 1997.

Cannistraci, David. *Apostles and the Emerging Apostolic Movement: A Biblical Look at Apostleship and How God Is Using It to Bless His Church Today.* Ventura: Gospel Light Publications, 2001.

Chodhrie, Victor. "The Training of House Church Leaders." In *Nexus: The World House Church Reader*, edited by Rad Zdero. Pasadena, CA: WCL, 2007.

Clowney, Edmund P. *The Church*. Leicester: IVP, 1995.

Coenen, L. "Kirche." In *Theologisches Begriffslexikon zum Neuen Testament*. Translated by L. Coenen, E. Beireuther, and H. Biedenhand. 3rd edition. Wuppertal: Brockhaus, 1972.

Compendium of the Social Doctrine of the Church. Online. http://www.vatican.va/roman_curia/pontifical_councils/justpeace/documents/rc_pc_justpeace_doc_20060526_compendio-dott-soc_en.html (Last access: 1 Oct 2015).

Dahl, S. "Einführung in die Interkulturelle Kommunikation." Online. http://www.intercultural-network.de/einführung (Last access: 19 June 2013).

De Cruchy, J. W. *Christianity and Democracy*. Cape Town: David Philip, 1995.

Demarest, Bruce A. *General Revelation: Historical Views and Contemporary Issues*. Grand Rapids: Zondervan, 1982.

Demina, N. A. *Andrei Rublev i chudozhniki yego kruga*. Moskva: Nauka, 1972.

Diettmann, Karsten. "Diakonie zwischen Kirche und Gesellschaft." Online. http://www.holmespeare.de.

D'Souza, Joseph, and Benedict Rogers. *On the Side of the Angels: Justice, Human Rights and Kingdom Mission*. Colorado Springs, CO: Authentic, 2007.

Escobar, Samuel. *La Palabra: Vida de la Iglesia*. El Paso: Baptist Spanish Publishing, 2006.

Esler, P. F. *Community and Gospel in Luke-Acts: The Social and Political Motivations of Lucan Theology*. Cambridge: University Press, 1989.

———, ed. *Christianity for the Twenty-first Century*. Edinburgh: T&T Clark, 1998.

Evans, M. *Prophets of the Lord*. London: Paternoster, 1992.

Ewert, David. *Holy Spirit in the New Testament*. Scottdale: Herald Press, 1983.

Faix, Tobias, et al. *Tat. Ort. Glaube*. Transformationsstudien, Vol 6. Marburg: Francke, 2014.

Farrar, Robert. *Kingdom, Grace, Judgement: Paradox, Outrage and Vindication in the Parables of Jesus*. Grand Rapids: Eerdmans, 1985.

Fee, Gordon. *Der Geist Gottes und die Gemeinde*. Erzhausen: Leuchter Verlag, 2005.

Ferraro, Gary. *Cultural Anthropology: An Applied Perspective*. Independence: Wadsworth, 1998.

Flückinger, F. "Das Wesen biblischer Prophetie." In *Zukunftserwartung in biblischer Sicht*, translated by Gerhard Meier. Wuppertal: Brockhaus, 1983.

Freedman, D. N., ed. *The Anchor Bible Dictionary*. Vol. 1, A–C. New York: Doubleday, 1992.

Freitag, Walter. "Vom Sinn der Weltmission." *EMZ* 1 (1950).

Gangel, Kenneth O., ed. *Team Leadership in Christian Ministry*. Chicago: Moody Press, 1997.

Garrisson, David. *Church Planting Movements*. Richmond, VA: Office of Overseas Operations International Mission Board of the Southern Baptist Convention, 2004. https://de.scribd.com/document/73786524/David-Garrison-CPM-Booklet.

Gensichen, Hans-Werner. *Glaube für die Wel: Theologische Aspekte der Mission*. Gütersloh: Mohn, 1971.

Gladis, George. *Leading the Team-Based Church*. San Francisco: Jossey-Bass, 1999.

Gnilka, Joachim. *Theologie des Neuen Testaments*. Herders theologischer Kommentar zum Neuen Testament. Supplementband. Freiburg-Basel-Wien: Herder, 1991.

Goppelt, Leonhard. *Theologie des Neuen Testaments*. Göttingen: Vandehoeck & Ruprecht, 1978.

Gornick, Mark R. *To Live in Peace: Biblical Faith and the Changing Inner City*. Grand Rapids: Eerdmans, 2002.

Gourdet, S. "Identification in Intercultural Communication." *Missionalia* 24, no. 3 (1996): 399–409.

Grudem, Wayne. *Systematic Theology: An Introduction to Biblical Doctrine*. Grand Rapids: Zondervan, 2004.

Hahn, Friedrich. *Theologie des Neuen Testaments*. Vol. 2. Tübingen: Mohr-Siebeck, 2002.

Hallencreutz, Carl F. *Kraemer towards Tambaram: A Study in Hendrik Kraemer's Missionary Approach*. Uppsala: Almquist & Wiksells, 1996.

Hardmeier, Roland. *Kirche ist Mission: Auf dem Weg zu einem ganzheitlichen Missionsverständnis*. Schwarzenfeld: Neufeld Verlag, 2009.

Hay, Ian M. *Isaiah and the Great Commission: An Old Testament Study of New Testament Missions*. Charlotte, NC: SIM, 1994.

Hedlund, Roger E. *A Biblical Theology of the Mission of the Church in the World*. Grand Rapids, MI: Baker Book House, 1985.

Heinrich, Wolfgang. *Building the Peace: Experiences of Collaborative Peace-building in Somalia 1993–1995*. Uppsala: Life & Peace Institute, 1997.

Hesselgrave, David J. *Communicating Christ Cross-Culturally: An Introduction to Missionary Communication*. Grand Rapids: Zondervan, 1991.

Hiebert, Paul G. *Anthropological Insights for Missionaries*. Grand Rapids: Baker, 1985.

———. "Are We Our Others Keepers." In *Integral Mission: The Way Forward*. Edited by C. V. Matthew, 196–220. Tirruvala, Kerala: Christava Sahitya Samithi, 2006.

———. *The Gospel in Human Contexts: Anthropological Explorations for Contemporary Missions*. Grand Rapids, MI: Baker, 2009.

Holland, J., and P. Henriot. *Social Analysis: Linking Faith & Justice*. Marknoll, NY: Orbis, 1983.

House, Paul R. *Old Testament Theology*. Downers Grove: IVP Academic, 1998.

Hughes, Philip E. *The Second Epistle to the Corinthians*. The New International Commentary on the New Testament. Grand Rapids, MI: Eerdmans, 1962.

Hunter, George G. III. *How to Reach Secular People*. Nashville: Abingdon Press, 1992.

Hybels, Bill. *Courageous Leadership*. Grand Rapids: Zondervan, 2002.

Ilyin, M. A. *Isskustvo moskovskoi Rusi Feofana Greka und Andreya Rubleva*. Moskva: Isskustvo, 1976.

Kaiser, W. *Mission in the Old Testament: Israel as Light to the Nations*. Grand Rapids, MI: Baker, 2000.

Kane, Herbert. *Wanted: World Christians*. Grand Rapids, MI: Baker, 1989.

Karecki, M. "Teaching Missiology in Context: Adaptations of the Pastoral Circle." In *The Pastoral Circle Revisited: A Critical Quest for Truth and Transformation*, edited by F. Wijsen, P. Henriot, R. Mejia, 159–173. Nairobi: Paulines, 2005.

Käser, Lothar. *Fremde Kulturen: Eine Einführung in die Ethnologie*. Bad Liebenzell: VLM, 1997.

Kirk, J. Andrew. *What Is Mission? Theological Exploration*. London: Darton, Longman & Todd, 1999.

———. *Mission Under Scrutiny: Confronting Current Challenges*. London: Darton, Longman & Todd, 2006.

Kittel, Gerhard, Gerhard Friedrich, Geoffrey W. Bromley. *Theological Dictionary of the New Testament*. Abridged in one volume. Grand Rapids: Eerdmans, 1985.

Klaiber, Walter. *Ruf und Antwort: Biblische Grundlagen einer Theologie der Evangelisation*. Gütersloh: Gütersloher Verlagshaus, 1990.

Klassen, Sarah, ed. *Lithuania Christian College: A Work in Progress*. Winnipeg: Leona DeFehr, 2001.

Knell, Marion. *Families on the Move: Growing Up Overseas – and Loving it!* Grand Rapids, MI: Monarch Books, 2001.

Köstenberger, Andreas J., and Peter T. O'Brien. *Salvation to the End of the Earth: A Biblical Theology of Mission*. Downers Grove, IL: InterVarsity, 2001.

Kraemer, Hendrick. *The Christian Message in a Non-Christian World*. Reprint in Missiological Classics Series, Vol. 6. Edited by Siga Arles. Bangalore: Center for Contemporary Christianity, 2009.

Kreider, Alan. "Mission and Violence: Inculturation in the Fourth Century – Basil and Ambrose." In *Mission in Context: Explorations Inspired by J. Andrew Kirk*. Edited by John Corrie and Kathy Ross, 201–216. Farnham, Surrey: Ashgate, 2012.

Kritzinger, J. N. J. "Black Theology – Challenge to Mission." Unpublished DTh, Pretoria, SA: Unisa, 1988.

———. "Who Do They Say I Am?" In *An African Person in Making: Festschrift for Prof. Willem Saayman*. Pretoria: UNISA Press, 2001.

Kümmel, Hans-Georg. *Die Theologie des Neuen Testaments nach seinen Hauptzeugen Jesus, Paulus, Johannes*. Göttingen: Vandehoeck & Ruprecht, 1976.

Kuzmic, Peter. "Justice, Mercy and Humility." In *Justice, Mercy & Humility: Integral Mission and the Poor*. Edited by Tim Chester. London: Paternoster, 2002.

Ladd, George Eldon. *Jesus and the Kingdom*. New York, NY: Harper & Row, 1964.

———. *A Theology of the New Testament*. Grand Rapids: Eerdmans, 1974.

Legrand, L. *Unity and Plurality: Mission in the Bible*. Maryknoll, NY: Orbis, 2002.

Lewis, R., and R. Wilkins. *The Church of the Irresistible Influence.* Grand Rapids: Zondervan, 2001.

Lingscheid, Rainer, and Gerhard Wegner, eds. *Aktivierende Gemeindearbeit.* Stuttgart-Berlin-Köln: Kohlhammer, 1990.

Loewen, Jacob A. *Culture and Human Values: Christian Interpretation in Anthropological Perspective.* Pasadena, CA: WCL, 1977.

Lohfink, Gerhard. *Wie hat Jesus Gemeinde gewollt?* Freiburg-Basel-Wien: Herder, 1982.

Losski, Vladimir. *In the Image and Likeness of God.* New York, NY: SVS Press, 1997.

Luther, Martin. "Schmalkaldische Artikel." In *WA BSKL* 50: 250.

Marshall, I. Howard. *New Testament Theology.* Downers Grove: InterVarsity, 2004.

———. "Who Were the Evangelists?" In *The Mission of the Early Church to the Jews and Gentiles.* Edited by Jostein Adna and Hans Kvalbei, 251–264. Tübingen: Mohr-Siebeck, 2000.

Martin, Ralph P. *2 Corinthians.* Word Biblical Commentary, Vol. 40. Waco, TX: Word Books, 1986.

Mayers, Marvin K. *Christianity Confronts Culture.* Grand Rapids: Zondervan, 1981.

McNeal, R. *Missional Communities: The Rise of the Post-Congregational Church.* San Francisco: Jossey-Bass, 2011.

Meyendorff, John. *A Study of Gregory Palamas.* London: Faith Press, 1964.

Moltmann, J. *Theologie der Hoffnung.* München: Chr. Kaiser Verlag, 1966.

———. *Theology of Hope: On the Ground and Implications of a Christian Eschatology.* New York: Harper & Row, 1967.

———. "Einführung: Einige Fragen der Trinitätslehre heute." In *In der Geschichte des dreieinigen Gottes. Beiträge zur trinitarischen Theologie.* München: Kaiser, 1991.

———. "Die einladende Einheit des dreieinigen Gottes." In *In der Geschichte des dreieinigen Gottes. Beiträge zur trinitarischen Theologie.* München: Kaiser, 1991.

———. *The Way of Jesus Christ: Christology in Messianic Dimensions.* Minneapolis: Fortress Press, 1993.

———. *Experiences in Theology: Ways and Forms of Christian Theology.* Translated by M. Kohl. Philadelphia: Fortress Press, 2000.

Müller, H. P. "Qahal Versammlug." In *THAT.* Translated by Ernst Jenni. Vol. 2, 609–619. München: Kaiser Verlag, 1979.

Müller, Karl, and Theo Sundermeier, eds. *Dictionary of Mission: Theology, History, Perspectives.* Eugene, OR: Wipf & Stock, 2006.

Müller, Wolfgang. *Dionysios Areopagites und sein Wirken bis heute.* Dornach: Pforte Verlag, 1990.

Murray, Stuart. *Church Planting: Laying Foundation.* Carlisle, Cumbria: Paternoster, 2001.

Myers, Bryant. *Walking with the Poor: Principles and Practices of Transformational Development.* Maryknoll, NY: Orbis, 2011.

Newbigin, Lesslie. *The Open Secret.* Grand Rapids, MI: Eerdmans, 1978.

Nolan, A. *God in South Africa: The Challenge of the Gospel*. Cape Town: David Philipp, 1988.

Ogden, Greg. *Unfinished Business: Returning the Ministry to the People of God*. Grand Rapids: Zondervan, 1990.

Osborne, Grant. *Romans*. Downers Grove: InterVarsity, 2004.

Ott, Craig, Stephen J. Strauss, and Timothy C. Tennent. *Encountering Theology of Mission*. Grand Rapids, MI: Baker, 2010.

Padilla, René. *Mission between the Times: Essays on the Kingdom*. Grand Rapids: Eerdmans, 1985.

Paffenholz, Thamia. *Community Based, Bottom-up Peace-Building*. Uppsala: Life & Peace Institute, 2003.

Payne, D. F. "The Meaning of Mission in Isaiah 40–55." In *Mission and Meaning: Essays Presented to Peter Cotterell*, edited by T. Lane Billington and M. Turner, 3–11. Carlisle: Paternoster, 1995.

Pentecost, Edward C. *Issues in Missiology: An Introduction*. Grand Rapids: Baker, 1982.

Peters, George W. *A Biblical Theology of Missions*. Chicago, IL: Moody Press, 1972.

Polunin, V. A. *Mirovozreniye Andreya Rubleva*. Moskva: Moscow University Press, 1974.

Ramseyer, Robert L., ed. *Mission and the Peace Witness: The Gospel and Christian Discipleship*. Scottdale: Herald Press, 1979.

Reimer, Johannes. "Mission des frühen russischen Mönchtums." Unpublished DTh thesis. Pretoria, SA: UNISA, 1994.

———. *Ende einer Suppermacht*. Basel: Brunnen Verlag, 2009.

———. *Liberty in Confinement: Faith Story in the Red Army*. Winnipeg: Kindred Press, 2000.

———. "The Spirituality of Andrei Rublev's Icon of the Holy Trinity." In *Acta Theologic*. Supplementum 11 (2008): 166–18.

———. *Die Welt umarmen. Theologie gesellschaftsrelevanter Gemeindearbeit*. 2nd edition. Marburg: Francke Verlag, 2013.

———. "Der Dienst der Versöhnung – bei der Kernkompetenz ansetzen: Zur Korrelation von Gemeinwesenmediation und multikulturellem Gemeindebau." In *Theologisches Gespräch* Heft 1 (2011): 19–35.

———. "Common Ground oder doch nur Anknüpfungspunkt? Zur Frage der hochspektralen Kontextualisierung am Beispiel des Islam." In *Theologie im Kontext von Biographie und Weltbild*. Tobias Faix/Hans-Georg Wünch/Elke Meier, 211–236. GBFE Jahrbuch 2011–2012. Marburg: Francke, 2012.

———. *Hereinspaziert: Willkommenskultur und Evangelisation*. Schwarzenfeld: Neufeld, 2013.

———. *Leben. Rufen. Verändern: Chancen und Herausforderungen gesellschaftstransformativer Evangelisation heute*. Transformationsstudien Vol. 5. Marburg: Francke Verlag, 2013.

Roloff, Jürgen. *Die Kirche des Neuen Testaments.* NTD. Ergänzungsreihe 10. Göttingen: Nandehoeck & Ruprecht, 1993.

Ross, M. G. *Community Organization: Theory and Principles.* New York: Harper, 1955.

Rusaw, Rick, and Eric Swanson. *The Externally Focused Church.* Loveland, CO: Group, 2004.

Saayman, Willem. *Christian Mission in South Africa.* Pretoria, SA: University of South Africa, 1991.

Samuel, Vinney, and Chris Sugden. *Church in Response to Human Need.* Oxford: Regnum, 1987.

Schaller, Lyle E. *Kirche und Gemeinwesenarbeit: zwischen Konflikt und Versöhnung.* Gelnhausen, Berlin: Burkhardthaus-Verlag, 1972.

Scharrer, Matthias, und Jochen Hilberath. *Kommunikative Theologie: Eine Grundlegung.* Mainz: Grünewald, 2002.

Schnackenburg, R. *Der Brief an die Epheser.* EKK, Vol. 10. Zürich/Einsiedeln/Köln: Benzinger/Neukirchener, 1982.

Schnee, Renate. "Gemeindewesenarbeit." Online. http://www.telesozial.net/cms/uploads/tx_kdcaseengine(scriptum_Gemeinwesenarbeit_Renate_Schnee_102004. pdf.

Schulten, Martin. "Gesellschaftstransformativer Gemeindebau. Am Beispiel der Evangelischen Freien Gemeinde Brüchermühle und deren Sozialarbeit für Hartkernarbeitslose in der Christlichen Beschäftigungsgesellschaft." Unpublished MTh dissertation. Pretoria, SA: UNISA, 2012.

Schultz, Richard. "Und sie verkündigen meine Herrlichkeit unter den Nationen. Mission im Alten Testament unter besonderer Berücksichtigung von Jesaja." In *Werdet meine Zeugen,* translated by Hans Kasdorf und Friedemann Walldorf, 33–53. Neuhausen-Stuttgart: Hänssler, 1996.

Schwarz, Fritz, and Christian Schwarz. *Überschaubare Gemeinde.* Gladbeck: Aussaat, 1980.

Scobbie, Charles H. "Israel and the Nations: An Essay in Biblical Theology." *Tyndale Bulletin* 43, no. 2 (1992): 283–305.

Senior, D., and C. Stuhlmueller. *The Biblical Foundations of Mission.* Maryknoll, NY: Orbis, 1983.

Scott, Waldron. *Bring Forth Justice.* Grand Rapids: Eerdmans, 1980.

Stott, John R. W. *New Issues Facing Christians Today.* Grand Rapids: Zondervan, 2006.

Sturm, Stephen. "Funktion und Leistung. Systemtheoretischen Analysen zur Sozialtheologie von Johann Hinrich Wichern." Online. http://mitglied.lycos.de/stephan_sturm/marburg2htm (Last access: 23 August 2017).

Suess, Paolo. "Zur Prophetie im Horizont der Menschenwürde." In *Mission und Prophetie in Zeiten der Interkulturalität,* translated by Mariano Delgado and Michael Sievernich. FS zum hundertjährigen Bestehen des Internationalen

Instituts für missionswissenschaftliche Forschungen 1911–2011. St Ottilien: EOS Verlag, 2011.

Sundermeier, Theo. "Konvivenz als Grundstruktur ökumenischer Existenz heute." In *Ökumenische Existenz Heute* 1 (1986): 49–100.

———. *Was ist Religion? Religionswissenschaft im theologischen Kontext.* Gütersloh: Gütersloher Verlagshaus, 1999.

Sundkler, Bengt. "Jésus et les païens." In *Contributions à l'étude de la pensée missionaire dans le Nouveau Testament.* Arbeiten und Mitteilungen aus dem neutestamentlichen Seminar zu Uppsala VI. Uppsala, Sweden: Neutestentliches Seminar zu Uppsala, 1937.

Sweet, Leonhard I. *Soul Tsunami: Sink or Swim in the New Millenium Culture.* Grand Rapids: Zondervan, 1999.

Tacke, H. *Glaubenshilfe als Lebenshilfe.* Neukirchen-Vluyn: Neukirchener Verlag, 1975.

Teague, Dennis. *Culture – the Missing Link in Missions.* Manila: OMF Literature, 1996.

Teinonen, S. A. *Missio poliica ecumenica.* Helsinki: The Finish Society of Missionary Research, 1961.

Tennent, Timothy C. "Followers of Jesus (Isa) in Islamic Mosques: A Closer Examination of C-5 'High Spectrum' Contextualization." *International Journal of Frontier Missions* 23, no. 3 (July–September 2006): 101–115.

Turner, Max. *The Holy Spirit and Spiritual Gifts Then and Now.* Grand Rapids: Baker Academics, 1996.

Ubeivolk, Vladimir. "Interviews with the Leadership of LttW and BoL." Unpublished paper. Chishinew: Archives of LttW, 2015.

Urry, James. *Mennonites, Politics and Peoplehood: Europe-Russia-Canada 1525–1980.* Winnipeg: University of Manitoba Press, 2006.

Van Engen, Charles. *Mission on the Way: Issues in Mission Theology.* Grand Rapids: Baker Academic, 1996.

Verkuyl, Johannes. *Inleiding in de nieweste Zendingswetenschap.* Kampen: Kok, 1975.

Vicedom, Georg. *Missio Dei – Actio Dei.* Nürnberg: VTR, 2002.

Volf, Miroslav. *After Our Likeness: The Church as the Image of the Trinity.* Grand Rapids: Eerdmans, 1998.

Von Stuckrad, K., ed. *The Brill Dictionary of Religion.* Brill: Leiden, 2006.

Walter, Manfred, trans. *Religion und Politik. Zu Theorie und Praxis des theologisch-politischen Komplexes.* Baden-Baden: Nomos, 2004.

Watson, David. *Gemeindegründungsbewegungen.* 2nd edition. Schwelm: DiM, 2011.

Watson, David, and Paul Watson. *Contagious Disciple Making: Leading Others on a Journey of Discovery.* Nashville, TN: Thomas Nelson, 2014.

Wendland, Heinz-Dietrich. *Die Briefe an die Korinther.* NTD Band 3. Göttingen: Vandehoeck & Ruprecht, 1976.

West, Charles C. "The Russian Orthodox Church and Social Doctrine: A Commentary on Fundamentals of the Social Conception of the Russian Orthodox Church."

Occasional Papers on Religion in Eastern Europe 22, no. 2 (2002), Article 3. Online. http://digitalcommons.georgefox.edu/ree/vol22/iss2/3 (Last access: 23 August 2017).

Wilckens, Ulrich. *Theologie des Neuen Testaments*. Vol. 1/1. Neukirchen-Vluyn: Neukirchener Verlag, 2002.

———. *Theologie des Neuen Testaments*. Vol. 1/3. Neukirchen-Vluyn: Neukirchener Verlag, 2005.

Williams, M. J. *The Prophet and His Message: Reading Old Testament Prophecy Today*. Phillipsburg: P&R Publishing, 2003.

Wright, Christopher. *The Mission of God: Unlocking the Bible's Grand Narrative*. Downers Grove: IVP Academic, 2006.

Wright, N. T. *Bringing the Church to the World*. Minneapolis: Bethany House, 1992.

Yoder, John Howard. *The Politics of Jesus*. Grand Rapids: Eerdmans, 1972.

———. *The Original Revolution: Essays on Christian Pacifism*. Scottdale: Herald Press, 1972.

———. *The Priestly Kingdom: Social Ethics as Gospel*. Notre Dame: University of Notre Dame Press, 1984.

———. *Politik Jesu – der Weg des Kreuzes*. Maxdorf: Agape, 1981.

Ziemer, Jürgen. *Seelsorgelehre. Eine Einführung für Studium und Praxis*. Göttingen: Vandenhoeck & Ruprecht, 2000.

Author Index

Subject Index

Scripture Index

NEW TESTAMENT

micah
global

He has shown you, O man, what is good. And what does the Lord require of you?
To act justly and to love mcery and to walk humbly with your God. Micah 6:8

Micah's Vision

Communities living life in all its fullness, free from poverty, injustice and conflict.

Micah's Mission

Rooted in the Gospel we become agents of change in our communities by being:

- **Catalysts** for transforming mission by promoting and living out **integral mission**
- A **movement** that advocates for poverty reduction, justice, equality, reconciliation and safety and wellbeing for all
- A **network** providing a platform for shared learning, collective reflection and action, inspiration and mobilisation of the Church, and the demonstration of Integral Mission.

Why Does Micah Exist?

Micah exists to be a catalyst, a movement and a network for **transforming mission**, with a special focus on enabling a united response to reducing poverty, addressing injustice and enabling reconciliation and conflict resolution.

We believe that Jesus came to give life in all its fullness (John 10:10). We believe that God has called out his church (*ecclesia*) to be his body, his representatives, his servants and demonstrate the new Kingdom in word and deed. We call this **integral mission**.

To learn more about Micah Global see: www.micahglobal.org
Find us on Facebook: www.facebook.com/MicahNetwork
Follow us on Twitter: @MicahGlobal
Enjoy our Instagram: www.instagram.com/micahglobal

Micah Global

PO Box 381, Carlisle, CA1 9FE, United Kingdom
Email: info@micahglobal.org
Phone: +44 1228 231 073

Langham
PARTNERSHIP

Langham Literature and its imprints are a ministry of Langham Partnership.

Langham Partnership is a global fellowship working in pursuit of the vision God entrusted to its founder John Stott –

to facilitate the growth of the church in maturity and Christ-likeness through raising the standards of biblical preaching and teaching.

Our vision is to see churches in the majority world equipped for mission and growing to maturity in Christ through the ministry of pastors and leaders who believe, teach and live by the Word of God.

Our mission is to strengthen the ministry of the Word of God through:
- nurturing national movements for biblical preaching
- fostering the creation and distribution of evangelical literature
- enhancing evangelical theological education

especially in countries where churches are under-resourced.

Our ministry

Langham Preaching partners with national leaders to nurture indigenous biblical preaching movements for pastors and lay preachers all around the world. With the support of a team of trainers from many countries, a multi-level programme of seminars provides practical training, and is followed by a programme for training local facilitators. Local preachers' groups and national and regional networks ensure continuity and ongoing development, seeking to build vigorous movements committed to Bible exposition.

Langham Literature provides majority world preachers, scholars and seminary libraries with evangelical books and electronic resources through publishing and distribution, grants and discounts. The programme also fosters the creation of indigenous evangelical books in many languages, through writer's grants, strengthening local evangelical publishing houses, and investment in major regional literature projects, such as one volume Bible commentaries like *The Africa Bible Commentary* and *The South Asia Bible Commentary*.

Langham Scholars provides financial support for evangelical doctoral students from the majority world so that, when they return home, they may train pastors and other Christian leaders with sound, biblical and theological teaching. This programme equips those who equip others. Langham Scholars also works in partnership with majority world seminaries in strengthening evangelical theological education. A growing number of Langham Scholars study in high quality doctoral programmes in the majority world itself. As well as teaching the next generation of pastors, graduated Langham Scholars exercise significant influence through their writing and leadership.

To learn more about Langham Partnership and the work we do visit **langham.org**

www.ingramcontent.com/pod-product-compliance
Lightning Source LLC
Chambersburg PA
CBHW072013090426
42740CB00011B/2172